7-07

"I'm ecstatic that Shaunti's extensive research about the inner lives of men has been translated for our younger generation. This is a phenomenal book that I wish I'd had as a teenager!"

—SHANNON ETHRIDGE
Bestselling author, *Every Young Woman's Battle*

"One of the top questions I get from teen girls is, 'Do guys think about us as much as we think about them?' Or how about, 'What's really going on in that brain of his?' Shaunti Feldhahn will help you crack the code to the male mystery in *For Young Women Only*. I only wish it had been around when I was a teenager!"

—VICKI COURTNEY
Founder of VirtuousReality.com, national speaker, and bestselling author of *TeenVirtue: Real Issues, Real Life…A Teen Girl's Survival Guide*

"Girls, this book is a MUST read! Shaunti and Lisa show you the basis of all good relationships between guys and girls. Get a head start for a successful marriage."

—CANDACE CAMERON BURE
Actress, speaker

"*For Young Women Only* provides a much needed in-depth look inside the hearts and minds of today's teenage boys. Whether you are a mom confused with your son's behavior or a teen girl seeking to understand your male peers, Shaunti provides a biblical framework for understanding, relating to, and appreciating our young men."

—REBECCA HAGELIN
Author, *Home Invasion: Protecting Your Family in a Culture That's Gone Stark Raving Mad*

shaunti feldhahn
and lisa a. rice

for young
women only

Multnomah Books

FOR YOUNG WOMEN ONLY
published by Multnomah Books
A division of Random House, Inc.
Published in association with Calvin W. Edwards,
Post Office Box 88472, Atlanta, GA 30356
© 2006 by Veritas Enterprises, Inc.
International Standard Book Number: 1-59052-650-3

Cover design by StudioGearbox.com
Cover photo by Robin Nelson
Interior design and typeset by Katherine Lloyd, The DESK, Sisters, Oregon

Unless otherwise indicated, Scripture quotations are from:
The Holy Bible, New International Version © 1973, 1984 by International
Bible Society, used by permission of Zondervan Publishing House
Other Scripture quotations are from:
Holy Bible, New Living Translation (NLT) © 1996. Used by permission
of Tyndale House Publishers, Inc. All rights reserved.
New American Standard Bible® (NASB) © 1960, 1977, 1995
by the Lockman Foundation. Used by permission.

Multnomah is a trademark of Multnomah Publishers
and is registered in the U.S. Patent and Trademark Office.
The colophon is a trademark of Multnomah Publishers.
Printed in the United States of America

For information:
MULTNOMAH PUBLISHERS
12265 ORACLE BOULEVARD, SUITE 200 • COLORADO SPRINGS, CO 80921
Library of Congress Cataloging-in-Publication Data
Feldhahn, Shaunti Christine.
For young women only / by Shaunti Feldhahn and Lisa Rice.
   p. cm.
ISBN 1-59052-650-3
1. Teenage girls--Conduct of life. 2. Teenage girls--Sexual behavior. 3. Man-
woman relationships--Religious aspects--Christianity. 4. Interpersonal relations
in adolescence. 5. Sex differences. I. Rice, Lisa Ann. II. Title.
BJ1681.F38 2006
248.8'33--dc22   2006013984

06 07 08 09 10—10 9 8 7 6 5 4 3 2 1

To our precious children

From Lisa:

To Sarah and Hannah—beautiful daughters and delightful friends, and Brandon—a great young man in training.

From Shaunti:

To a wonderful young lady and little laddie, who in a few short years will grow into a strong and godly young woman and man.

Contents

Chapter 1

WHAT IN THE WORLD ARE THESE GUYS THINKING?

Have you ever wondered what the guys you hang out with are really thinking and feeling? Has your boyfriend ever completely shut down on you, leaving you wondering why a totally minor incident ticked him off so much? Do you ever find yourself wishing that the cute but untalkative guy in class would open up a bit more?

Would it matter if you understood the unique way guys are wired?

Whether you're reading this book for fun, curiosity, or out of desperation to understand guys, we believe you will come away with a brand-new perspective on how guys think that will affect your life in high school, college, and beyond.

SIX INSIGHTS

This chart shows the six insights the book is going to cover. These six "surprises" help us move past our surface understanding (what we assume about guys) and take us inside to what these guys are really feeling at their core.

Our Surface Understanding:	What That Means in Practice:
Guys need respect.	Guys would rather feel unloved than inadequate and disrespected.
Guys are insecure.	Although guys look confident—even cocky at times—they are often insecure in themselves. They worry that they will be found out, and therefore are drawn to girls who help them feel like they measure up.
Guys are tough and indestructible.	Guys look indestructible, but on the inside their hearts are tender, easily hurt, and strongly guarded. However, they will let down their defenses when they know their heart will be safe with a girl.
Guys are visual.	Even decent guys in great dating relationships struggle with the desire to visually linger on and fantasize about the female body—and much of that struggle depends on what a girl is wearing.
Guys are all out for one thing.	Teenage guys are conflicted by their powerful physical desires, which also have massive emotional consequences. Guys need your help to protect both of you.
Guys go after the hot girls.	Guys are attracted to girls with a good personality as well as inner and outer beauty, but they can't force a physical attraction.

So where did we get this information?

The short answer: from the guys themselves.

The longer answer: In 2004, Shaunti wrote a book called *For Women Only: What You Need to Know About the Inner Lives of Men*. That little book explained a bunch of things that women just tend not to "get" about men, and it became a bestseller. It's been talked about on TV and radio, and Shaunti has had speaking engagements about it all across the country.

People started asking Shaunti for a follow-up book that would teach the same concepts, but in a way that would better relate to you as teenagers. They wanted answers to the question: What don't young women already know about guys that they really need to know?

> Where did we get this information?
> From the guys themselves.

We figured this need was a no-brainer. What teenage girl wouldn't *love* to have some previously undiscovered insight into what guys are really thinking and feeling?

So we began our research—and discovered that getting teenage guys to honestly share their deepest needs and fears wasn't easy. We eventually hit on the right formula, and held lots of confidential meetings (focus groups) with groups of teen- and college-age males—and conducted informal interviews with guys everywhere. We also did a ton of test surveys, stopping guys in malls, in coffee shops, and on the street. When we promised the guys that their names would never be revealed, many of them overcame their usual fear of baring their souls. And, wow, did we learn some fascinating things!

The survey

We hired several experts to help us test whether everything we'd been learning by just talking to guys was true. They helped us design and conduct a scientific survey of four hundred guys from all over the country who were between the ages of fifteen and twenty to see how they *really* thought and felt about a bunch of different things.*

For Young Women Only is all about the guys' fascinating answers from that survey and all those interviews. Because it's a short book, instead of trying to cover everything, we are focusing on things that girls tend not to "get" about guys. We've divided our findings into the six insights on the chart, all of which are backed up by statistical evidence. Each chapter of the book will cover one of those six insights. We think you'll be amazed by some of the surprises, just like we were.

---

* The survey polled 404 guys ages fifteen through twenty, with roughly even numbers in each age bracket. The survey was completed only by guys who were living within the United States, and (because this is a book about relationships with girls) who were heterosexual.

Two for the price of one

Occasionally we also include some survey results or quotes from *For Women Only* (FWO). That survey included men all over the country from ages twenty-one to seventy-five and was followed up with informal interviews of many more. We've included a little of that information because sometimes it helps to see what guys will be like a few years down the road. So really, you're getting the benefit of two surveys and two books for the price of one!

> When we promised guys their names would never be revealed, we learned some fascinating things!

Hearing it from the horse's mouth

The best and most important part of hearing the truth about guys *from* guys is that it helps us really know and believe it's true.

In this book we want to move you from the place of *wishing* certain things about guys to *knowing the truth* about them—right from their own mouths. And when you know the truth, you will have the opportunity to make better, smarter decisions about how you interact with the guys you know. Hopefully, those new choices will help you as you relate to your guy friends, boyfriend, and even family members.

Your guides to the male brain

So who are we? There are actually two people writing this book. There's Shaunti, who wrote *For Women Only*. For that book, Shaunti did tons of research and data gathering about men that no one had done before. Turns out, her Harvard graduate degree and years as a Wall Street analyst helped pave the way for these well-researched books!

> We want to move you from the place of wishing certain things about guys to knowing the truth about them.

Then there's Lisa, a screenwriter, author, and editor for several magazines and books. Along with her writing expertise, Lisa brings her practical experience of raising teenagers. Her daughters, Sarah and Hannah, have helped her tremendously, including rolling their eyes and editing out any hopelessly "uncool" things they read in the first draft.

Neither of us is a counselor, so we have drawn on the expertise of counselors, youth workers, pastors, and others who work with and understand teens. The best experts in this book, however, are the hundreds of guys your age. We hope they will make you laugh while teaching you a lot about what it means to be a guy.

BEFORE WE START: GROUND RULES

Before you turn the page and get a look at the inner lives of guys, here are some ground rules:

1. First, you may have noticed that the media often makes fun of guys and stereotypes them. We won't be doing that here. We honor the guys who shared their hearts with us, and believe that you will really appreciate their insight.

2. Second, this is not an equal treatment of male-female differences. We don't deal at all with how guys can or should relate to *you*. Yes, girls obviously also have needs, and many of the truths discussed in these pages apply to you too. But since the theme is the inner lives of *guys* and our space is limited, we're focusing entirely on how girls relate to guys, not the other way around.

3. Third, remember that there are always exceptions to every rule. When we say that "most guys" appear to think a certain way, realize that "most" means exactly that—most, not all. Since we have limited space in these pages, go to www.foryoungwomenonly.com to explore more resources, read the entire survey, or join the discussion on these issues.

4 Fourth, we're talking about what is *normal* inside guys, not necessarily what is *right or wrong* about their outward behavior. We want you to understand their thoughts and feelings, even when we may not agree with their actions.

5 Fifth, we need to warn you that some of the enclosed insight may be hard to hear. In all honesty, we were tempted to exclude certain points. But we realized that we were hearing important things that the guys themselves often can't say directly to the girls they know. So we decided to trust you with this information. If anything is distressing to hear, please don't wrestle with it alone. Please pray about it and talk about it with an older woman you can trust.

> ❀ We're talking about what is normal inside guys, not necessarily what is right or wrong about their outward behavior.

6 Finally, as we discuss these findings, from time to time we'll be looking at the results from a faith perspective, especially when there are noticeable differences between the answers of guys who say they don't have any particular religious beliefs, and those who do. The nationally representative survey included all types of guys, regardless of their personal beliefs, and we think this information will be helpful even if you look at life and faith differently than we do. But we believe that adding the faith perspective is also valuable as we consider what to do with all this new information.

By letting you in on the guys' secrets, we hope you will take it as an opportunity not just to learn fascinating new things, but also to practice new ways of relating. Not only can you become a much better girlfriend (or a much more attractive prospect!), but it's a lot easier to learn good habits now in your teen relationships, so you don't have to break bad habits later when you are married!

In other words, the point of learning this new information is not to change the guys in our lives, but to change and improve *ourselves*.

So, sit back and relax—and maybe fasten your seat belt!—as we take you on a journey into the inner lives of guys.

Chapter 2

YOUR LOVE IS *NOT* ENOUGH

You Mean He Wants My Respect More Than My Love?

Guys would rather feel alone and unloved than inadequate and disrespected.

In the middle of writing this book, I (Lisa) was babysitting Shaunti's young children, who were spellbound by the movie *The Incredibles*. The villain—Syndrome—becomes a cruel bad guy just because he wants respect and hasn't gotten it. His whole life is about getting revenge, simply because, as a boy, he was brushed off and not respected.

Not long after watching that movie, I went to a semi-final state football game between rival high schools in our area. Among the wild, noisy fans, I noticed one guy's team T-shirt. It said, "Loved by few...hated by many...respected by all...The Brookwood Broncos."

There was that word again...*respect*. Clearly, for this football fan, it wasn't about being loved, and it was even okay to be hated...but boy, he wanted that respect! What is it about respect that's so important to a guy?

> It wasn't about being loved, and it was even okay to be hated...but boy, he wanted that respect!

More important, could it be true in the real world (beyond movies and sports) that respect carries so much weight? We discovered that the answer is *yes*—and that this one fact creates a bunch of ideas for you to think about, as a girl...and down the road, as a woman.

RESPECT VERSUS LOVE

Just after college, I (Shaunti) watched something amazing unfold at a singles' retreat. For the very first session, the retreat speaker divided the room in half and placed the guys on one side, and the girls on the other. "I'm going to ask you to choose between two bad things," he said. "If you had to choose, would you rather feel alone and unloved in the world *or* would you rather feel inadequate and disrespected by everyone?

I remember thinking, *What kind of choice is that? Who would ever choose to feel unloved?*

The speaker then turned to the guys' side of the room. "Okay, men. Who here would rather feel alone and unloved?"

A sea of hands went up, and a giant gasp rippled across the girls' side of the room.

> What is it about respect that's
> so important to a guy?

He asked which guys would rather feel disrespected, and the girls watched in bewilderment as only a few guys lifted their hands.

Then it was our turn to answer and the guys' turn to be shocked when most of the girls indicated that if they had to, they'd rather feel inadequate than unloved.

WHAT IT MEANS

While it may seem odd to most of us, the male need for respect and affirmation—especially from the main girl in his life—is even more important than love. The survey indicated that *two out of three guys* agreed that they'd prefer to be unloved—just don't make them feel inadequate! And the importance of respect only increases as the guys grow into men.

Take a look at the survey results.

SURVEY SAYS:

Think about what these two negative experiences would be like: to feel alone and unloved in the world OR to feel inadequate and disrespected by everyone. If you were forced to choose one, which would you prefer? Would you rather feel...?

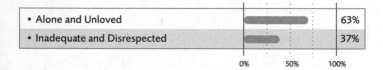

• Alone and Unloved	63%
• Inadequate and Disrespected	37%

0%   50%   100%

This need for respect actually becomes stronger as the guys get older—74 percent of the adult men in the *For Women Only* survey valued respect more than love. Look at these comments teen guys made about that survey question:

● "I'd rather be alone and unloved. For a guy, being disrespected is just not right. *I'd rather be by myself than have someone disrespect me.*"

● "Most guys—teens through young twenties—would rather feel respected than loved. Respect makes us feel adequate in every part of our lives, whereas with love...well, we have our whole lives to find that special person to love."

We girls, on the other hand, tend to be more motivated by and tuned in to love over respect—and we're often better at showing love than showing respect. Have you ever done something to make a guy feel loved and been disappointed by his response? Maybe without knowing it you were also making the guy feel disrespected. (And that, by the way, automatically makes guys feel unloved, too.) If you want to love your guy in the way *he* needs to be loved, you need to make sure that he feels your respect most of all.

> "I'd rather be alone and unloved. For a guy, being disrespected is just not right."

HIS BRAIN IS ON YOU!

During our focus groups, we heard over and over that guys spend most of their time trying to get *your* attention and respect! The people around him—most especially you, as a girl—are almost like a mirror. He's looking to you in the hope of seeing something respectable about himself, something that will make him feel strong and trustworthy.

During one focus group, the guys were asked, "What percentage of your waking hours is spent trying to impress girls?"

It took a half-second for one guy to respond: "About a hundred." Another admitted that everything he did—from the way he dressed to the car he purchased to the job he took—involved a consideration of what a girl would think about it. Would she approve and think it was a good choice? Would she respect him because of it, or would it cause her to think less of him?

As he talked, all the other guys around the circle were nodding in forceful agreement. I (Lisa) was sitting in this group and had to work to keep the surprise out of my face. If you're anything like me, you may not have realized just *how* important it is to guys to have the respect of the girls they care about—or how painful it is when they don't feel they have it. In fact, if they sense they are not respected, they'll be looking for the door. One college guy told us:

> When a girl respects you, it makes you wake up and
> say, "I can do better than this other girl I'm dating,
> who doesn't seem to feel the same way." If girls around
> you are treating you with respect but you're not get-
> ting it from your own girlfriend, a lightbulb goes on.

If respect really is their highest need, it makes perfect sense that they will gravitate toward girls who make them feel that way—and run from those who don't.

A disrespect-o-meter

Here's the problem: In our focus groups, guys clearly believed that girls *know* when they're disrespecting them. But even long-married women—much less teenage girls—often really *don't* realize that that is what they are communicating!

In fact, most of us probably *do* respect the guys closest to us, but we don't realize when our words or actions are saying the opposite. However we sure do get blindsided by the results! For example, have you ever been totally confused at why a guy got upset during a conversation?

> ✳ If they sense they are not respected, they'll be looking for the door.

Many guys have a tough time expressing their feelings, and so they can't always explain *why* they are upset. But thankfully, there is a way to know when we've crossed the disrespect line: Watch for *anger*.

Consider this: If you are in an emotional fight or conflict with the most important guy in your life, do you think it is okay for you to cry? Most of us would probably answer *yes*. Now consider this: In that same conflict, do you think it's okay for the guy to get really angry? Most of us have a problem with that—we think he's out of line.

But Dr. Emerson Eggerichs, founder of Love and Respect Ministries, has a different view: "In a relationship conflict, crying is often a woman's response to feeling unloved, and anger is often a man's response to feeling disrespected."

Most guys won't blurt out something like "You're disrespecting me!" in the heat of the moment. But rest assured, if he's angry at something you've said or done and you don't know why, there is a good chance that he is feeling the pain or humiliation of your disrespect.

In the survey, two-thirds of the teenage guys who described themselves as being in longer-term relationships said that in a conflict they were most likely to be feeling disrespected. We girls are far more likely to be wailing, "He doesn't love me!"

SURVEY SAYS:

In the middle of a conflict with a girl, I am more likely to be feeling...

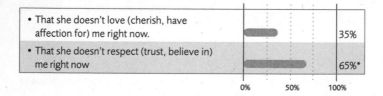

• That she doesn't love (cherish, have affection for) me right now.	35%
• That she doesn't respect (trust, believe in) me right now	65%*

0%　　　50%　　　100%

(*Among guys who are in committed or longer-term relationships. Even including guys not in a relationship, the overall average of those answering "she doesn't respect me" was still 57%.)

In the *FWO* survey, the percentage of men saying they'd probably be feeling a lack of respect shot up to 81 percent.

> If he is angry, he may be feeling the pain of your disrespect.

Unconditional respect

Do you think you can't or shouldn't respect a guy until he's earned it? That's a common assumption. But think about this: If you are in a serious relationship with a guy, don't you want him to love you unconditionally, even when you're not being particularly lovable? Well, guys feel the same way about respect. They know that they will make mistakes in life, and they are really hoping and looking for someone who will demonstrate that she respects them, regardless of whether they're meeting her expectations at the moment.

"We've become such a love-dominated culture," Dr. Eggerichs says. "Like the Beatles said, 'All you need is love.' So we've come to think that love should be unconditional, but respect must be earned. Instead, what men need is *unconditional respect*—to be respected for who they are, apart from how they do."

If you, as a young woman, learn how to treat guys with

respect right now, these attitudes and habits will carry over into your marriage one day. In a famous Bible passage on marriage, Ephesians 5 never tells the wife to love her husband, and it never tells the husband to respect his wife. That's probably because we each already tend to give what we want to receive. Instead, over and over, it urges the husband to *love* his wife and urges the wife to *respect* her husband.

> "What men need is unconditional respect—to be respected for who they are, apart from how they do."

Thinking ahead

Obviously, there is a difference between marriage and dating. There's also a difference between being in a committed boyfriend-girlfriend relationship and being "just friends." When we talk about learning to unconditionally show respect, it is with an eye toward the context of Ephesians 5, which is not dating, but *marriage*.

The applications of this truth change as a relationship becomes more committed. We are *not*, for example, suggesting that you "demonstrate respect" by brushing aside obvious concerns about a guy's character in order to date someone you might not be able to trust. We *do* believe that when you read this book—just like most of the adult women who read *For Women Only*—you will discover that you have a lot of room to grow and learn about how to care for and respect the guys in your life.

So now that we know respect is so important to guys, and that they think we already understand exactly what we are doing in the area of respect, what are we going to do about it?

So now that we know respect is so important to guys, what are we going to do about it?

WHAT DOES RESPECT LOOK LIKE TO A GUY?

In the movie *A Walk to Remember*, the aimless, moody, reckless Landon Carter's (Shane West) life changes when he's forced to do a school play and draw on the help of the serious, conservative preacher's daughter, Jamie (Mandy Moore). Although Jamie has a lot of intense and hidden things happening in her own life, she shows that she is unique among all the girls by encouraging Landon to follow his passions. Her encouragement eventually draws him out of his shell and into life.

At the beginning of the story, after Landon has made an immature, costly decision, it just takes one look from Jamie to shame him and challenge him to change. At the end, when Landon makes a selfless decision, the look on Jamie's face says how proud she is of him. She challenges him and makes him feel he can conquer his demons and become the man he was intended to be.

I hope you are getting a sense of what *power* girls have in the lives of guys. God has given each of us the ability to either tear a guy down or build him up. Assuming that we want to use this gift wisely—never for selfish gain—how do we actually *do* it?

In the *FWO* survey, we were amazed at how important it was to men that the women in their lives respected them in several different ways, including respecting their judgment and abilities. But in relationships between young people, there are three areas that are most important. And they all have to do with communication. Sometimes it's even a matter of what we *don't* say.

1. What we say in front of others

Do you ever tease a guy in front of your friends? Or jokingly put him down in a group setting? Would you believe that can be torture for him? One teenager said:

Girls don't realize how easily they can embarrass us. And when you're embarrassed, you don't want to say anything. Honestly, I get mad; I just don't show it. But as soon as we're in private, I say, "Why did you do that? Couldn't you wait until another time?" And it's worse if it's in front of her friends because they'll all talk about it later. It's terrible. I'm thinking, *Do other girls that don't even know me also think that?*

Good-natured teasing is a light example, but there is actually a pretty serious epidemic of public disrespect for men. It starts with the way they are portrayed in television, movies, and other media, but it doesn't end there. Dozens of guys shared how painful it was to be criticized by girls in public, to have their judgment questioned in front of others.

One guy said, "The male ego is the most fragile thing on the planet. Women have this thought that *He's got such a huge ego that I need to take him down a peg*. No way. The male ego is incredibly fragile."

A twenty-year-old single guy said:

If another guy tries to knock you down a peg, you have fallbacks. You can say, "Well, I'm smarter, I can whip your tail, I've got a better car..." But when a girl puts you down, you don't really have come-backs. You don't think about how you're better than girls, so when a girl does that, it's devastating. There's no notch to go to unless you get nasty, and you don't want to do that with a girl. You just get angry, instead.

Females often think of this as male pride—but that isn't it. What is at stake isn't his pride as much as his secret feelings of inadequacy as a guy. There's a big difference between feeling prideful and feeling adequate.

> ✳ There's a big difference between feeling prideful and feeling adequate.

2. How we say it

Some things just push a guy's buttons. Often, it's not *that* we say something, but *how* we say it. In our interviews, a lot of guys said something like this: "When a girl says something disrespectful, I often think, *I can't believe she doesn't know how that makes me feel!*" We had to reassure these guys over and over that the girls probably didn't *mean* to disrespect them and were likely just clueless.

So what are the guys hearing?

Hearing disrespect

One of the older guys we interviewed, who had just graduated and started life in the working world, described how women are often viewed in the automotive industry—simply because of how they phrase their requests or "suggestions":

> In the man world if you want to get something done—repaired, printed, built—if you will respect the man and be polite, everything will open up for you. If a woman says to a mechanic, "I have a few questions, but I trust your judgment; you're the best and that's why I brought you my car," her chances of being cheated drop dramatically. But, if she comes in with a "princess-diva-I expect bad things" attitude and makes a bunch of demands, everything will suddenly get very expensive and go in slow motion.

In the above situation, I'm guessing the "diva" was just trying to be assertive about what she wanted so she didn't get taken. However, because she was dealing with *guys*, she didn't realize that she needed to intentionally express her confidence in the man while making her requests. The guy took it as a disrespectful demand—and no doubt, he took his sweet time on her car.

Hearing disappointment

Many males read something negative into even a simple female reminder or question.

One high schooler said that when his female class-project partner asked him, "Have you not started the PowerPoint presentation yet?" he found himself getting angry—even though she didn't ask it in an accusing tone. He said, "After all, I told her I would do it. The deadline was still days away and I felt like she had no trust that I would find a way to get it done. She should know I'm not an idiot. She didn't need to act all suspicious and disappointed."

Now remember, girls, all she'd asked was, "Have you not started the presentation yet?" Was she suspicious and disappointed? I doubt it, but that is what he heard in her question! Again, it wasn't what she was saying—he had no problem with her checking up on a joint project—but *how* she was saying it.

One guy put it this way:

You have to realize: Guys have a built-in desire to save the damsel in distress. They don't want to be used, but most men will go out of their way for a lady.... We'll change your flat in a blinding snow-storm, and we'll carry furniture upstairs in 95 percent humidity if you ask nicely. A woman of any age can ask a guy age twelve to age ninety-nine, and if they ask nicely, the guy will melt. But if she doesn't act grateful and respectful, we've lost our motivation.

Wow! Guys are in agreement on this one. They say that even if a girl has a knowledge of what's wrong, or needs to make a suggestion, if she's careful and polite in the way she presents it, she'll get a lot farther with her goals. For example, "How's the PowerPoint project coming along?" assumes that he's doing it and makes it easier for him to say honestly where he is.

3. Respecting his opinion

A guy deeply needs the girls in his life—especially a potential or actual girlfriend—to respect his opinions and decisions. No one wants a girl to pretend to be clueless, but many guys wish their girlfriends wouldn't question their knowledge or argue with their decisions all the time. Look at these comments from teen guys:

- "I dated a girl who nagged me and questioned me constantly…'You never do this,' 'You never take me out,' 'Why did you buy this old Honda?' She just ragged on me all the time. But she didn't realize that finances were already a huge burden for me.

When she slammed me with questions and expectations like that, I felt so inadequate. And that is just a terrible feeling for any guy."

- "To a certain point, I don't mind being questioned—because if a girl questions the way I do things, as long as she sees why I did it, she can trust me next time. But then when the next time comes and if she still can't trust me, and it's a pattern, it's not worth my time to be questioned over and over again. It all plays back into taking my word for it...respecting that my decisions will be for the ultimate good."

Several guys confessed that they felt like their opinions and decisions were actively valued in every area of their lives *except* with the girl they most wanted that from! Some guys felt that their buddies at school or work trusted their judgment more than their girlfriends did. Some felt that their girlfriend was even ordering them around—something that didn't even happen with their parents, or their boss!

Because we females are created differently, we often don't understand that something that seems minor to us can actually be a big deal to a guy. A guy might think of it like this: "If she doesn't trust me in this small thing, she sure wouldn't trust me in anything big—so she probably doesn't really trust me at all."

SO WHAT SHOULD WE DO?

Girls, you hold incredible power—and responsibility—on this issue. You can either strengthen guys or tear them down in ways that go far beyond your relationship with them. Every area of a guy's life is affected by whether or not he gets respect from the people he cares about. A guy's inner feelings of personal adequacy are the foundation for how he approaches the world. That's why guys are so drawn to girls who they can tell honestly respect and admire them. Those are the girls, the guys told us, that they are far more likely to be interested in.

> ✳ God has given each of us the ability to
> either tear a guy down or build him up.

So what should we do? As one guy put it, "Always assume the best and you will find it easier to show respect." Simple as it sounds, choose to demonstrate respect and choose *not* to demonstrate disrespect.

We can choose to demonstrate—by words and actions—how proud we are of our guys and how much we trust them. Just as we love to hear "I love you," a guy's heart is powerfully touched by a few simple words: "I'm so proud of you" and "I trust you." And when we realize that we've blown it, we can acknowledge our fault and ask for forgiveness. The guys recommended saying something like, "I'm sorry I did that—that sounded disrespectful. I know I can trust you."

> "Always assume the best and you will find it easier to show respect."

It's only going to get more important...

Girls, we hope you will keep in mind that over the next few years, the guys you know will increasingly value respect over love. Most of all, they will want to feel respected by the woman who will be their wife. One of the men from the *FWO* survey said:

> You know that saying "Behind every good man is a great woman?" Well, that is *so true*. If his wife is supportive and believes in him, he can conquer the world—or at least his little corner of it. He will do better at work, at home, everywhere. By contrast, very few men can do well at work *or* at home if their wives make them feel inadequate.

As you learn, <u>think</u>

As you learn, remember that earlier word of caution. Yes, learn respectful patterns of relating to guys, but don't put your own brain into neutral while you do it.

The guys around you have a growing need to feel that you trust them, but they are also *growing* in trustworthiness—and the Bible only discusses that full and unconditional respect in the context of marriage. So in any casual or dating relationship, you need to be discerning. Be thoughtful...and careful! As you now have glimpsed, inside their confident exterior many guys are very vulnerable and even insecure. That is the subject of the next chapter.

Chapter 3

THE PERFORMANCE
OF A LIFETIME

Mr. Gorgeous and Cocky
Is Actually Insecure?

*Although guys look confident, they are often
insecure in themselves, worry that they will be
found out, and are therefore drawn to girls
who help them feel like they measure up.*

Have you ever seen a movie with the British actor Patrick
Stewart? He's got a commanding presence, and I (Shaunti)
will admit that I particularly loved him as the confident
Captain Jean-Luc Picard in *Star Trek: The Next Generation*.
In one episode, the captain and his friend Dr. Beverly
Crusher are (of course) stuck on a dangerous and unfamiliar
planet. And their predicament has an interesting twist:
Because of some unwanted alien meddling, the two can hear
each other's thoughts.

As the captain tries to lead them toward help, he scans

41

the unfamiliar horizon, motions in a particular direction, and says, with his usual commanding certainty, "This way." But remember: The female doctor can hear what he's thinking—and he's just been busted! She stares at him and says, "You don't really know, do you? You're acting like you know exactly which way to go, but you're only guessing!" Then, with growing amazement, she asks, "Do you do this all the time?"

He gives her a look, then answers. "There are times when it is necessary for a captain to give the appearance of confidence."

THE REALITY BEHIND THE CONFIDENCE

Beverly Crusher had just discovered what many of us never grasp—that most guys are hiding a deep inner uncertainty. Even the most confident-seeming guy dreads the moment when he will be exposed for who he really is—or at least believes himself to be: an impostor.

"They are going to find me out!"

One nineteen-year-old put it this way: "Guys do pretend sometimes, hoping we're right. We take guesses and make it appear we know what we're doing…hoping we can figure it out later!"

❀ Most guys are hiding a
deep inner uncertainty.

And don't think this is just youth and inexperience talking. We heard the *exact same things* from grown men surveyed for *FWO*. A lot of males carry around this belief that they are fooling everyone and are going to be "found out"—even if they really are perfectly capable of doing whatever it is that they are insecure about.

SURVEY SAYS:

"Regardless of how successful you are in school, athletics, and activities (or your career), which statement best describes your feelings about your performance in these areas?"

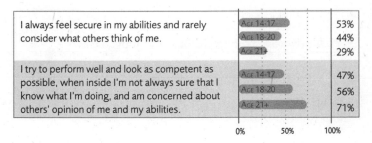

	Age 14-17	Age 18-20	Age 21+
I always feel secure in my abilities and rarely consider what others think of me.	53%	44%	29%
I try to perform well and look as competent as possible, when inside I'm not always sure that I know what I'm doing, and am concerned about others' opinion of me and my abilities.	47%	56%	71%

Notice that over just a few short years, the older the guys get, the more likely they are to feel (or admit to) this inner insecurity and the need to look confident. Perhaps the stakes seem higher with age—or perhaps the younger guys are just less likely to admit to that insecurity!

One college guy said:

Teens have the biggest egos. From ages seventeen to twenty-one, at least some of us have the "I can do anything and get away with it" mentality. But as we hit the real world we become more realistic—and more insecure—about our abilities and who we are as a person.

What does this feel like for him?

There seem to be three recurring thoughts that are furiously racing around inside the cool, collected, confident-looking guys you know:

- "I'm always being watched and judged."

- "I have no idea how to do this."

- "But I *want* to do this!"

"I'm always being watched and judged."

A guy's inner vulnerability about his performance is made more intense by his belief that at all times he is being watched and judged…and perhaps found wanting. One guy put it this way: "We think about what others think about us *all the time*."

Look at this example from one recent college graduate:

Even though I'm all grown up now and run my own business, at church I'm still just the little kid who they remember playing drums and getting into mischief. Sometimes even at my *business*, people will come and say things that make me suspect they still view me as that immature kid. They start joking around in this environment where I'm trying to get others to look up to me, and I'm thinking, *Okay, this is not the time. Go away.*

This secret male vulnerability isn't just a concern about what others think of them. It also includes the knowledge that since they *don't* always know what they are doing, they are just one mess-up away from being found out.

> "We think about what others think about us all the time."

One high schooler said, "No one else knows you don't know what you're doing. You seem calm under pressure, when inside you're confused as all get out." And as our surveys found, this sense of uncertainty becomes more pronounced as the guys get older and face more challenging real-world situations.

"Think of some times in the last few years when you've faced unfamiliar and challenging situations. Which of these feelings were you most likely to experience? (This is not about how you acted, but how you felt.)"

I can handle it; no problem.	Age 15-20	46%
	Age 21+	26%
I'm not 100% sure that I know exactly what I'm doing, and I hope it doesn't show.	Age 15-20	54%
	Age 21+	74%

0%   50%   100%

"I have no idea how to do this."

Of course while everyone is watching, many guys are hiding the fact that they really *aren't* sure what they are doing. Another recent college grad told this story:

> Last summer some friends were getting married, and I filmed their wedding. I had no real idea what I was doing. In one way, I loved the challenge, but the

entire time I was also going, *Act like you've been there. Act like you've been there.* But the truth is, I was just making it up as I went along.

Another guy said, "I may be smiling and nodding, but in the back of my mind I'm thinking, *I have no earthly idea how to do this, and I hope I can learn it before they find out.*"

"But I want to do this!"

The comment of the "wedding video guy" above hints at the flip side to a guy's inner insecurity: the hunger for a challenge, something new and exciting. These two feelings may seem contradictory, but they are all part of the male make up. Males want to conquer Everest, but they also know they'll have to risk taking a humiliating tumble on the way.

As you might guess, those times are when guys feel the shakiest and need the most encouragement from us.

HOW DO WE SPOT IT?

A guy who is secretly feeling insecure in himself is probably not going to tell you! So how do we spot it?

The guys clued us in to three signals of insecurity: bravado, humor, and "faking it."

Boys and bravado

> *Bravado:* (bruh-VA-doh) A pretense of courage;
> a false show of bravery. —Dictionary.com

Many guys bragged about how they always felt secure in themselves—which is a sure sign that they *don't* feel real secure. Check out this exchange from one of our high school focus groups:

Guy #1:   I always feel secure…always.

Guy #2:   You do not, man. Be honest. How about your golf game?

Guy #1 (standing and advancing toward Guy #2): Shut up!

In another group, one high school sophomore was really honest about this: "We try to look like we always know what to do, even though we don't. *That's why guys get mad when they're questioned.*"

Males want to conquer Everest, but they also know they'll have to risk taking a humiliating tumble on the way.

Who's the clown?

Many guys revert to humor when something happens to throw them off balance. Look at these quotes:

- "If I screw up, I just make people laugh. I turn it around into something funny, and it's okay. For example, if I give the wrong information in class and everyone laughs, I can either stand there and be humiliated, or I can take a bow."

- "There's almost nothing you can't get out of with a little humor. If you're not so brilliant about a certain subject, you can cover by just making the teacher laugh...becoming the class clown who competes with the class brain. At least then you feel good at *something*."

Just fake it, man!

Just as common as humor, we found that guys become masters at "faking it." This is not the same thing as bravado. As one guy put it, this is "Looking calm, cool, and collected while on the inside going, *Oh man, I hope I can figure this out before they see right through me!*"

One college guy told us:

In sports, a guy will try to fake it as long as possible. He'll say, "Sure, I can golf." But when he gets out there, he can tell they're watching him, trying to figure him out. Ninety-five percent of guys would never admit to not knowing how to do something, not being able to perform. He'll try to hide it.

Another guy said, "I'll try just about anything, knowing that I've either got the basic skills or I can fake the skills until I get it."

Now, obviously, it is going to be pretty difficult to spot when a guy is faking it. The point here is that just because a guy looks totally confident in himself, don't assume that he always *is*.

WHEN FAKING IT FAILS

So how do guys feel when they *can't* hide their insecurities or cover their mistakes with humor?

One guy put it this way. "You feel inadequate—like you're not worth anything. I get real scared that I'm not going to be able to excel. So if I fail a quiz, I'll just have to put on a front and keep my feelings inside. You don't want to let others know you're struggling."

Over and over, the guys told us that letting others see their struggles or mistakes simply didn't feel like an option. One seventeen-year-old guy told us a story that illustrates how difficult it is for teenage guys to risk embarrassment, even if they *know* that the benefits would outweigh any temporary humiliation:

> I play guitar and sing, and I take lessons from a phenomenal guitarist who's played with Cindy Lauper and the Spin Doctors. One night he was jamming with some equally great guys, and he called me over and asked me to join them! But here's the thing: Instead of jumping at it, I answered, "Oh, I'm sorry, I can't. My fingers hurt tonight. I'm tired…I have a big test in the morning…"—and I left, just so I wouldn't have to be embarrassed. But I could have really learned a *lot* if I had stayed.

Here's what it comes down to: For a guy, *the idea of someone thinking he can't cut it is humiliating—a feeling he wants to avoid at all costs.*

❄ Guys told us that letting others see their struggles or mistakes simply didn't feel like an option.

SEARCHING FOR SIGNALS

Guys are always looking to those around them for cues about whether their secret insecurity has any foundation or not. So how you respond to them—whether in flippancy, ridicule, or encouragement—has a great deal to do with how a guy will end up feeling about himself. There are three main places guys search for these signals: family, school/work/activities, and relationships—in other words, *you*.

Family

Obviously, the input of their mom and dad is an enormous factor in how they feel about themselves. Look at these two comments:

- "Parents are way up there. They can make or break a guy's confidence level."

- "My mom doesn't appreciate me, so it's tough. This week she said she wanted me to vacuum the whole house to get ready for company, and I did, but she never said thank you. She rarely points out the positive…. It stinks."

> ❀ Guys are always looking to those around them for cues about whether their secret insecurity has any foundation or not.

School/Work/Activities

Look at a story a high school senior told us:

> I was having a great semester last spring, but then, I had a brain freeze in physics. I went up to the board and kept plugging in the wrong formula for the speed of light. I asked my teacher about it and instead of getting objective answers—or help—I got a rant about my personhood. She said I was bright, but lazy. And that absolutely killed the rest of my week. Rather than taking the perspective of "Oh, that teacher is just a nag," I internalized it. After all, she didn't rant on my scholarly knowledge; she ranted on me, personally. That just killed me. No, I don't need the approval of everyone, but when someone smacks me down, I can't stand it.

We may think that a guy should *know* that the negative signals aren't true and not internalize them, but remember…they are *already* secretly worried that maybe it *is* true. One guy in a band put it this way. "Yeah, if I don't pass a musical audition, I don't think that the judge is unfair. I think that I suck at my instrument. And if I do poorly on a test, I'll think, *I can't believe it. I'm such a failure*—even if I typically do well."

This is particularly torturous when a guy has risked that dreaded humiliation to try something new—and is teased for it. Look at this guy's comment:

> This one time, I was invited to be in a commercial. I didn't realize, though, that everyone had to do fifties-style dancing around a jukebox. Just when I got up my nerve and tried some steps, the producer passed by me and offhandedly said, "Ya goofball!" That's all it took. I was completely off balance the rest of the day. Even now, it's humiliating to think that I probably looked like a total spaz.

Relationships

Since guys look to girls for signals, they are fearful about what girls might say—in other words, how girls might hurt them. One high school junior said, "Girls may be aware of the disrespectful things they say and do, but they think they can get away with it because we're strong. But on the inside, we're not as strong as they think we are."

Guys feel constant anxiety about how they're performing in front of girls. They doubt their desirability, their wit, and their ability to land the great girl. One guy said, "I'm always putting my foot in my mouth with a certain girl I like. I start stammering like a fool, when normally I'm a pretty articulate guy. I feel like Cody Banks when he's trying to talk to Hilary Duff, and it all comes out wrong."

In the movie *Agent Cody Banks*, Cody (Frankie Muniz) isn't happy until the Hilary Duff character affirms him. In his mind, he's not an okay person until he senses her approval. In our focus groups, many guys expressed similar feelings—that the girls around them send some of the most important signals about how they're doing in life.

> Guys feel constant anxiety about how they're performing in front of girls.

What about God?

Now let's push the pause button for a second. For those of us who believe God should be our primary source of approval, we may look at this and think, "Well, guys like that just need to get their affirmation from Him!" And yes, it's true that none of us can seek our primary sense of self-esteem from others. Our primary value comes from being beloved children of the King.

But that said, remember: God Himself was the one who said in Genesis, "It is not good for man to be alone"! God knew that man was incomplete without woman—even though God was there, too. The desire to be "completed" by a woman is formed by God into the heart of every man.

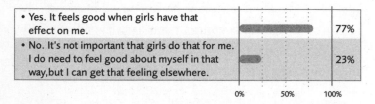

SURVEY SAYS:

"Do you want the girls in your life to help you feel like you measure up to what everyone expects of you—to feel like you're worthy of respect?"

• Yes. It feels good when girls have that effect on me.	77%
• No. It's not important that girls do that for me. I do need to feel good about myself in that way, but I can get that feeling elsewhere.	23%

0%   50%   100%

On the survey, three out of four guys emphasized how important this was. As one put it:

It's good when a girl makes you feel you measure up. It's the opposite of disrespect, which I hate. It makes you feel you're worth something, that you have what it takes, that she likes you and believes in you. One girl told me, "I respect you. I really look up to you and respect your opinion." That makes me feel like a man...like I can do anything.

Another guy pitched in: "It's a huge confidence builder. Makes me feel that my opinion counts and my words are really taken into consideration. It's awesome when girls ask for advice."

Almost every guy we talked to said they would rather hear encouragement from a girl than a guy! Look at this interchange from one focus group:

Guy #1: If I get a new haircut and I'm not so sure about it, and Bill or John says it looks good, that's fine. But it's not quite the same as when a girl says it.

Guy #2: It's 'cuz they're a girl, dude! It's awesome when they say it…they're *girls*!

> ❀ Almost every guy we talked to said they would rather hear encouragement from a girl than a guy!

Think about all the times you haven't been supportive of the guys you care about—simply because you didn't understand that they could possibly be feeling insecure. Sobering, isn't it?

WHAT SHOULD WE DO?

So what should girls do about this, if they want to be someone guys will gravitate toward…instead of someone they will avoid? Here are some comments from guys about what girls did that either tore them down or built them up.

What *not* to do...

- "The worst thing she can say to me is, 'Why haven't you done X today?' She's just proving, again, that I'm a failure."

- "Sometimes she says, 'I really don't feel loved right now. I wish you would do X, Y, or Z for me.' When she says that I feel like such a screwup. Man, I can't even make her feel appreciated! What's the point of cleaning up my act? It'll never be enough."

- "My worst thing is when we've had an argument and I do something nice and she says, 'I know why you're doing this.' I just can't win!"

- "Younger girls don't understand that you can't rag on a guy when he's down."

What to do: affirm him...

...to others:

- "If your girlfriend is complimenting you and bragging about you to your friends—or even to hers—and it gets back to you, it puts confidence in you. You know she's thinking about you and that she cares!"

- "I have to admit I love it when she brags about me to her friends."

- "Any bragging on you is great. It sends you soaring."

...to him:

- "It speaks volumes when a girl chooses to look at the good in me, even when she's upset. Part of respect is looking past the stupid circumstances and saying, 'How can we work this out?' My girlfriend's unselfishness in that way makes me want to be a better man. She makes me want to step up to the plate."

- "When I've finished playing my drums at a concert, and I walk off the stage, I see my girl standing there, smiling, and my heart skips a beat. She takes my arm and says to me, 'Oh, baby, you did good...you're the best,' and I'm on cloud nine for a week."

- "For me, my girlfriend is always out for my best interest. She gives me heartfelt friendship and support. She has no problem giving me a slap in the face, but it's okay because *I know she's always acting in my best interest.* I don't find elements of selfishness in her."

Bragging or affirming?

Okay, but isn't bragging wrong? Well, that's actually part of the issue: Guys know that it's wrong for them to brag on *themselves*—that shows a lack of humility. But when *you* tell them or someone else how wonderful they are, it's not usually prideful bragging but positive affirmation. (That's part of what the apostle Paul meant in his biblical letter to the Philippians, when he said to think about whatever is"excellent" or "worthy of praise!")

On the other hand, if a guy isn't convinced that his girl thinks he's the greatest, he will tend to seek affirmation elsewhere. He may spend more hours at work, hobbies, sports, or retreat to his computer. One guy asked us:

Why else do you think so many men take sports so seriously? It's something they feel good at, something they've practiced. They are admired and encouraged by other men on the field. People say "Good hit!" or "Good shot!" or show by tightening their defense that they know you're about to smoke them. There's nothing like that feeling.

What message are you giving the guys you care about?

THE GIFT OF CONFIDENCE

In the movie *Spider-Man 2*, we watch as Peter Parker tries to hold his complicated life together—and doesn't do a very good job of it. He's practically killing himself trying to rescue people at all hours, and at the same time juggling school, relationships, and a job. He ends up disappointing his professor, his boss, his landlord—and worst, the girl he secretly loves. They view him as a slacker, not knowing about his secret life. His secret love, Mary Jane, gets so fed up with him seeming to choose other things over her that she gets engaged to another man.

Peter's confidence drains away as he sees his worst fears and insecurities about himself unfold before his eyes. He gets more and more depressed as he disappoints one person after another. Finally, he can't handle it any more, and he gives up his superhero gig—until, of course, Mary Jane needs to be rescued.

At the end, she finds out the truth of who Peter is. And she astonishes him by choosing him over the other man. But although he's grateful, he still lacks confidence. He's given up being the superhero in order to protect his girl from disappointment or danger—but in doing so is not being the man he wants to be.

In the last scene, when Peter is finally kissing the girl of his dreams, he hears the city sirens that have so often beckoned him to drop everything and save the day. He turns away and smiles at Mary Jane with a look that says, "Don't worry; I'm choosing you."

But instead of clinging to him in selfishness or fear, she gives him one last kiss, nods toward the window and says, "Go get 'em, tiger." And off flies an exuberant Spider-Man, fully loved, fully confident now in being the hero that he wants so much to be.

What about you? What message are you giving the guys you care about? Is it a selfish message of, "You're not quite enough"? Or an encouraging message of, "Go get 'em, tiger!"?

The guys around you secretly want you to see them as a superhero, too. And if you show them that you do, you have the ability to help them overcome their secret insecurities and fly out into the world with confidence.

Chapter 4

TOUGH OR TENDER?

A Peek into the Real Heart of Mr. Tough Guy

Guys may look indestructible, but their hearts are tender, easily hurt, and strongly guarded. Yet they will let down their defenses when they know their heart is safe with you.

Imagine you are a time traveler from a long-gone era, and you have never seen a stove before. You see a large silver area on a countertop, with four circular elements on it—but you don't know what they are. One circle is black but the others are glowing red. You put your hand down on the black one, and it's fine. But when you touch the others you get your fingers scorched.

You quickly learn that these circles can be painful. So you either stay far away from them, or, if you must go near, you put on the Teflon oven mitt you find lying by the side of the stove. As a matter of fact, you find the Teflon mitt so protective that you wear it a lot—even if it's not strictly needed.

Guys often look like Teflon on the outside. Nothing seems to burn them. Stuff just slides off. But in reality they are just as easily hurt as you are.

"WE DO GET OUR FEELINGS HURT... WE JUST DON'T SHOW IT."

Although guys *look* emotionally indestructible, they aren't. They are instead very tender and easily hurt on the inside. In this chapter, you'll hear from the guys themselves just how much they feel the need to protect themselves emotionally.

All the guys we surveyed and talked to said they must develop a tough exterior in a world that can really hurt them if they let it. Especially since guys—unlike girls—feel that they are not "allowed" to show all those emotions that they are feeling inside. They've learned to keep their emotions to themselves.

> ✳ Although guys look emotionally indestructible, they aren't. They are instead very tender and easily hurt on the inside.

As one high school junior told us, "Guys are like this: We don't show emotions, but we're not emotionless. We do get our feelings hurt, but we don't show it because we want to be in control."

Why do guys hide their real feelings? It turns out there are three main reasons.

"Otherwise, I'm gonna get burned..."

Guys put up a tough front and keep emotions at bay primarily because they are tender and easily hurt. It's a way of protecting themselves. Of course, most guys would probably never put it that way if they weren't in an anonymous focus group! Several guys said, "Tell the girls reading your book that we get *angry*. Saying 'Guys get their feelings hurt' sounds so...so...*girly*!'"

Okay, fine: They get *angry*. But whether they put it in terms of anger or hurt or whatever, their hearts are a lot softer inside than they want to let on.

As one guy put it: "Vulnerability is a four-letter word."

A member of a school band said this: "Everyone's human, whether they let it show or not. Sometimes I have to be a role model in the band and show strength and leadership, but that doesn't mean I have no insecurities or problems."

And the guys have learned that they are most vulnerable with people that they care about. As one high schooler put it,

"The people you love the most can hurt you the most. If you don't care about someone and it feels like they betray you, it doesn't matter as much."

"It's just what's expected of me..."

Guys also purposely hide their emotions because they feel it's expected of them. It would feel weird not to, and others would think they were weak.

For instance, we heard: "If I'm having a bad day, I can't let it show. I've got to keep that smile on and that energy up." And, "If you feel awful on the inside, you won't let it show on the outside. I don't want to show my emotions, really...to let people know. I try to hide them—at least in public."

Even guys who are friends don't really open up to each other. Some do, but it's rare, as these comments illustrate:

- "If you're with a guy, and something's on your mind, it's like a game. You nod to each other, as if to communicate some sort of understanding. But it doesn't really cut it. We think that nod should do it, but it doesn't get it out. You just don't pour it all out to a guy because they usually get uncomfortable and don't really listen."

- "If a guy came to me with a girl problem, I might give him a quick, manly hug and pat him on the back real hard and tell him there are lots more fish in the sea."

● "You don't express your heart to guys…just the basics."

Whether they put it in terms of anger or hurt or whatever, their hearts are a lot softer inside than they want to let on.

"I just don't know how to do otherwise…"

Because they've been trained from childhood to suppress emotions, many guys sometimes don't actually know *how* to express what they are feeling. So they just don't say anything.

As one high school junior put it, "Guys are just as emotionally driven as girls, but there are a lot of emotions we just don't know how to express."

Guys are also very aware that because of that, they can come across as insensitive with girls. Most want to change that image. In one group, the conversation went like this:

Guy #1: "No real guy wants to hurt a girl's feelings…only jerks and idiots do that."

Guy #2: "The general population of guys looks like jerks and idiots, you idiot! That's why they're writing this book!"

THOSE RED-HOT BURNERS

Obviously, it wouldn't matter how vulnerable a guy was if there were no hot elements that could burn him—no girls ready and willing to chime in with hurtful words and actions.

One of our biggest surprises was the huge number of guys that didn't trust most of the girls they knew. They felt like the girls would hurt them, if they let them. Sure, they *like* girls, these guys said—but they wouldn't necessarily *trust* them.

Now, the guys said there was a difference between girls they "generally knew" (as we put it on the survey) and the few "best female friends" (or girlfriends) they let into their inner life. But of course the *reason* they let these girls into their confidence was that those girls had proven that they wouldn't burn them.

SURVEY SAYS:

"How often do you find yourself <u>not</u> sharing your inner feelings with girls you generally know? (This does NOT include your best female friend or girlfriend.)"

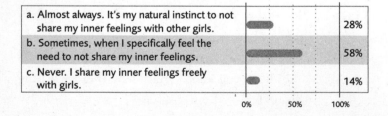

a. Almost always. It's my natural instinct to not share my inner feelings with other girls.	28%
b. Sometimes, when I specifically feel the need to not share my inner feelings.	58%
c. Never. I share my inner feelings freely with girls.	14%

Add it up: 86 percent of guys either *always* or *sometimes* withhold their inner feelings from girls.

Why?

SURVEY SAYS:

Is the following statement true or false? A main reason for not sharing your inner feelings is to protect yourself from getting hurt, and/or because you don't trust some girls to handle your personal information with care.

Yes, that's true.	68%
No, that's false.	32%

0%   50%   100%

As one guy put it, "I only tell my guy friends what's going on inside. It's too risky to tell a girl."

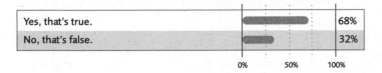

One of our biggest surprises was the huge number of guys that didn't trust most of the girls they knew.

Remember that although a guy may look like nothing bothers him, *he knows* that if someone emotionally cuts him, he will bleed. And we were surprised at the vast number of guys who felt like there were just a lot of sharks in the water—a lot of girls that they couldn't trust to handle their vulnerabilities with care and discretion. So, the guys said, they had learned to be tough instead.

"I only tell my guy friends what's going on inside. It's too risky to tell a girl."

One college guy—one of those seemingly tough jocks— told us this story:

I was very shy in high school. I know I probably looked like I wasn't, but I was. Even as a relatively "popular" guy, I was really insecure inside. I really liked this girl in my class, and wanted to go out with her, but I was just too chicken to call her and ask her out. So I had my best friend call her, just to test the waters, while I listened in on the extension. My buddy talked to her for a minute, and then said something like, "You know, I think my friend digs you—would you ever want go out with him?" Immediately, this girl said, "No, he's boring, he's not my type." I felt like she just stuck a dagger in my chest. It's been like, three years, and I can still remember exactly what she said, the exact words she used. It sounds stupid, but it's taken me years to recover from that.

If you think a guy's feelings can get hurt *only* by this sort of romantic rejection, think again. Remember, guys are secretly wondering whether they measure up in every area—not just in romance. So it is surprisingly easy to crush their feelings in many situations. One senior from a church youth group told us this story: "We were writing in our AP Language Arts class one semester, and this girl in my class got a 90 on her paper, where I got a 70. She turned to me and said, totally kidding, 'Ch...You're just not as good as me.' And I *know* she was kidding...but I was already bummed about the grade, so it really hurt."

Maybe you read that and think, *Well, that's silly. No guy should get hurt by something that minor.*

That's actually the point.

Guys are just made differently than we are. What we might think of as a stupid, side comment actually has the potential to hurt a lot. We aren't making these quotes up. When we were able to have confidential conversations with teenage guys, we heard story after story about how parents, teachers, and peers have "burned" the guys they care about through careless words or actions.

But especially devastating was the pain of being hurt by girls.

ARE GIRLS REALLY "MEAN GIRLS"?

Several of the guys commented on the 2004 movie *Mean Girls*. In the movie, as many of you know, a home-schooled child of zoologists, Cady Heron (Lindsay Lohan), enters school for the first time as a high school sophomore. Moving from Africa to America, she finds that the rules of the high school social pecking order are far scarier than anything she's known in the jungle. She makes friends with some less-popular students, but when she infiltrates the group of beautiful but backbiting "Plastics," she quickly discovers not only how mean these girls really are but how easy it is to become one.

One guy who brought up the subject said, "The movie is true. Girls are scandalous. They're driven by an agenda, and they'll stop at nothing to get what they want."

Believe it or not, we heard comments like that over and over, some of which we'll share shortly. Guys seem to feel this way about many girls—but is it accurate? Is it possible that some of the real-life girls might not actually be "mean" but just be perceived that way? Or if they are, how can they have their eyes opened to it, and change? We asked a couple with a lot of counseling experience to share their insight directly with you.

ASK THE EXPERTS: Clayton Kull, L.C.S.W., and Cheryl Kull, both Parents, Counselors, and Ordained Ministers

We are not surprised that many guys are confused, intimidated, or put off by girls who seem to be mean or controlling. It's a real problem—even in the church. Girls often *do* act that way because they believe it's the only way to get acceptance and attention. These girls will seduce, connive, deceive, manipulate, split, divide and conquer—all types of control—to make sure they will never be hurt again.

We have seen two types of controllers. Both are acting out of woundedness—although it may not always look like it. The first we'll call the "Jezebel," so named after the manipulative wife of King Ahab in the Bible. The Jezebel is subconsciously committed to conquering and destroying—but it's because she's been really hurt. Underneath, she's afraid of being abandoned. So she usually then finds the second type of girl, whom we'll call "the approval addict." This girl has also been wounded, but instead of being the aggressor, she falls prey to a "friend" like the Jezebel, who will build her up only to control her. To affirm their sense of self-worth, the Jezebel wants friends who look up to her, and the approval addict wants friends that she sees as "better than her."

Neither are healthy patterns, and they usually lead to acting in hurtful ways, which we will discuss a bit later.

Where do guys see mean girls?

We'll warn you that it may be hard to hear some of the following comments. Take a deep breath and review these not-so-flattering quotes from some guys about how they view girls in general—and realize we only put in a small percentage of the many, *many* comments we heard:

- "Girls are always trashing other girls...pretending to be their friend but talking behind their backs all the time. A guy won't do that: He'll say it to your face. But since we see the girls acting that way, we know: *beware*."

- "You can tell girls are not safe when you see how they treat each other. Guys will fight it out and resolve it, but girls aren't confrontational in an honest way. They're more like the mafia...'I'm gonna kill your mom, your dog, everyone.' They'll start rumors and get their posse together—like a scene from *Anchorman* or *Gangs of New York*, where no one knows what they're fighting about."

- "Girls can't trust each other with information. I hear stories about how a girl broke up with her boyfriend, and the friend she confided to about the breakup is going for her ex within two days. It's like anything's fair game with a girl."

"You can tell girls are not safe when you see how they treat each other."

- "Whenever a girl does something bad, it seems their whole gender is evil. I tell myself I'm just going to play video games the rest of my life. You fall back into testosterone land. It's like a limb just got broken."

- "Girls can work on an assumption about someone and then just *run* with it, even if they are wrong. I swear they listen to every third word."

So many of the guys said they wished they *could* let down their defenses and express themselves with girls. They enjoy and need the more emotion-based female perspective on life. They want good female friends. But in order to get that female perspective, guys have to make themselves vulnerable to rejection and getting burned—a difficult risk for them to take.

As one college guy put it, "Ego is one of the biggest things a guy has, and girls can destroy it easier than anyone."

Another one said, "It's far worse to be disrespected by a girl. You can handle it or write it off with a guy, but not with a girl.

When do guys feel hurt by girls—what do they see as "mean"?

As you have read to this point, you might be feeling defensive and even angry—or perhaps just surprised that guys think so many girls are "mean." We thought it would be helpful to give you an overview of the main things that guys said made them wary—the things they saw as "mean-girl stuff." You may think some of these comments are harsh, or that they aren't you at all…and maybe they aren't! But remember that we're not talking about how girls feel on the inside, but how girls may be perceived on the outside. And we're sure most of you would prefer to know the biggest concerns for guys, in case there *is* anything you might need to change.

> "It's far worse to be disrespected by a girl. You can handle it or write it off with a guy, but not with a girl."

Guys hate:

Being judged negatively: "I haven't gotten to the point where I can tell my girlfriend anything. I can tell my four best friends, knowing I won't be judged or looked down on. I hope to get to that point with my girlfriend. That would be the safest place. I'm not there now."

Having arguments: "I can't stand when we argue. She's faster than I am, verbally, and I feel trapped. I'm always thinking, 'What did I do to deserve that?'"

Deception: "I've been lied to and hurt so many times, I don't trust girls. I tell myself that the second someone else knows, it's not a secret. So I keep my inner thoughts to myself."

Gossip: "Girls talk too much. They go to the bathroom in groups of five, and they talk about stuff…like us. At least guys just react to negative stuff with their testosterone. Girls get evil, and do and say things behind your back."

Jealousy: "My girlfriend can be so suspicious and jealous of my time. One night I was working late, and she called to ask what I was doing. She kept asking questions like, 'When are you coming home?' 'Why do you have to work so late?' 'Why are you snapping at me?' I was excited to hear her voice when she first called, but after a few minutes I was screaming, 'Okay! I'll call you later!'"

Grudges: "Girls hold grudges and have a harder time forgiving. And they are patient about their grudges. They'll say to themselves, 'I'm going to ruin you, and it'll take two months.'"

And finally...

Meanness: We wish we could cut down the number of quotes to one—we wish there *was* only one quote on this subject! (Or none!) But since the guys absolutely overflowed with examples of perceived meanness among the girls they knew, we figured we should print a few more quotes:

- "Guys will give a quick jab, but girls will go for your heart."

- "Guys will take another guy down...but we won't ruin his reputation. Girls will."

- "I get confused with some girls because of how they talk. I can't discern sarcasm versus truth. Are they being nice, or mean? It's a minefield we're navigating."

Taking stock of where you are...

Is it possible that others see you that way? Let's check back in with our experts...

ASK THE EXPERTS: (...continued)

Could you be a "Jezebel"?

- Do you find yourself plotting to get back at someone who has wronged you?

- Do you know any girls who will pretty much do whatever you suggest that they do? ("Wednesday is pink day...")

- Do you find yourself getting annoyed with and wanting to exclude—or even subtly destroy—a formerly close friend, thinking that she no longer measures up?

Could you be an approval addict?

- Is there a "friend" you couldn't imagine yourself surviving without?

- Is there someone in your life that draws you in through shopping, gifts, phone calls, or flattery?

- Do you remain loyal to them even in the face of being disrespected, taken advantage of, and treated unkindly?

- Are you afraid to make a friend angry with you, fearing that she will reject you?

- Do you need someone else—besides God—to tell you you're okay?

If you recognized yourself in either the Jezebel or the approval-addict pattern, it's time to search your heart and work toward change. Remember, those patterns often start from being hurt—so if someone has rejected or abandoned you, choosing to truly forgive them can change everything. Also, ask God to forgive you for manipulating circumstances to meet your own needs, and for loving the benefits (approval, power, etc.) of the unhealthy relationship more than the benefits of trusting God. Ask Him to heal you, separate you from unhealthy people, and attract healthy people as friends. Then enjoy the process of a healing heart.

BECOMING THE GIRL
THEY WANT TO BE FRIENDS WITH

So if guys don't trust "mean girls," what's the alternative? Does every guy think all girls are horrible? Thank goodness, no!

Here's the good news: All the guys we talked to knew and admired many "safe" girls. Guys value these girls for being the kind of friends that are not just good, but truly *great* for a guy's heart. Guys let down their defenses with girls they *know* are safe.

There are millions of these girls out there. Maybe you're one of them. Or maybe you're great in some ways but, like most of us, still have a few things to learn.

> Guys value safe girls for being the kind of friends that are not just good, but truly *great* for a guy's heart.

So how *do* you become one of those safe girls? Just as we listed what the guys found unsafe, here's what they said was *great* about the girls they trusted:

Listen, understand, and affirm

Guys are looking for affirmation and understanding from girls, not competition.

- "I don't want her to be able to beat me in a wrestling match. I want her to listen, and know me, and understand what I'm going through."

- "If I blow it, my girl lets me know her feelings haven't changed…that I haven't let her down…that she's cheering for me."

- "If she'll ask me something, with sincerity, I'll open up and let her know where I am."

Make them feel great about themselves

- "The best thing is when she laughs at my humor."

- "If you hang out with girls that can make you laugh, it's better. It makes me feel more adequate. I want to find someone I know will make me feel adequate."

Be careful of others' feelings

Guys notice it when girls *don't* gossip. In one of the best sermons in the Bible, Jesus said, "The meek will inherit the earth." *Meekness* is basically "having the power to slice and dice but refraining." Wouldn't you love to have guys make one of these comments about you?

- "I've never heard that girl say an unkind thing about anyone."

- "She doesn't make jokes at the expense of others."

Relax and go with the flow

Guys want someone lighthearted. They appreciate girls who can go with the flow and let life happen:

- "I think it's great when a girl is secure enough to let you talk to other people, and not hold on to you for fear you'll leave her."

- "This one girl I like lets things roll off her shoulders. She doesn't freak out about every little thing."

> Guys let down their defenses with girls they know are safe.

Great power = great responsibility

We'll say it again: You have been designed with a unique power to build up the guy(s) in your life. And guys want this kind of help and support from you! Though the males around you may seem big and tough, remember there's a little boy inside each one who's easily hurt and looking for a safe place where he can be real.

Do you have any patterns that make you an unsafe friend? If you do, ask God's forgiveness. He wants to help you develop a pure heart that will bring life to others, not confusion and rejection.

It comes down to the Golden Rule: "Do unto others as you would have them do unto you." Do you want a friend? Then be a friend. Do you want a safe place for your secrets? Then be a secret-keeper. Do you want to be built up and affirmed? Then do the same for those you care about. We promise—it'll all come back to you in the end.

Chapter 5

KEEPER OF THE PHOTO FILES

What "Guys Are Visual" Really Means...and What It Means for You

> *Even decent guys in great dating relationships struggle with a desire to visually linger on and fantasize about the female body—and much of that struggle depends on what a girl is wearing.*

Recently I (Lisa) watched a *Seinfeld* rerun, where Jerry gets a notice that he owes the New York City Public library a bunch of money because he hadn't turned in a book back in the '70s. He's so mad because he specifically remembers turning it in, and the reason he remembers is that a certain girl was there with him. Jerry remembers the exact orange sweater she was wearing (twenty-five years earlier!) and that her figure caught his eye. He tells his friends that her image is forever seared in his brain.

In this episode, the Seinfeld writers touched on a powerful fact: what it means that guys are "visual."

Here's what that reality might look like in your world:

Scene One: Jon, an honor student, athlete, and musician in his junior year of high school, is sitting in his Trigonometry class on a normal fall day. The teacher asks a girl at the back of the class to come to the front and work out a problem on the whiteboard. The girl makes her way forward.

Amanda has a good figure, and she's wearing form-fitting shorts and a spaghetti strap shirt. She's not showing off her body—she's just wearing the usual clothes from A&F. She begins to work the problem, all business, seemingly unaware of the quiet stares.

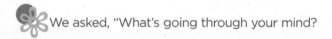 We asked, "What's going through your mind?

Scene Two: We're talking to a series of randomly selected teenage guys, many of whom are already dating other girls—and many that we know to be decent, trustworthy guys. We describe Scene One above and ask: "If you were Jon, what would be going through your mind as the girl works at the board?"

Here are some of their answers:

- "Nice body."

- "I hope she gets to work out *all* the problems on the board today."

- "I wonder what underwear she's wearing."

- (Next guy, overhearing) "...or if she's wearing underwear."

- "I'm thinking...is she a virgin?"

- "What's going through my mind?! No way am I telling you what's going through my mind! Let's just say it has nothing to do with math."

- "If I'm not careful, I might start wondering what she looks like with none of those clothes on."

- "Focus on the math. Do you want to graduate or not?"

- "If I'm not real careful, my memory would instantly be replaying a porn clip my older brother showed me when I was thirteen."

If you had been with us, listening to those guys, what would *you* be thinking? Would you be amazed? Disappointed? A little of both? Most girls who hear comments like these are a bit surprised—just as I (Shaunti) was when I first stumbled across this issue while researching *FWO*. Our first reaction is to think, "Oh man, those guys have a *serious* problem!" But we heard those sorts of comments even from great guys, godly guys who won't even let themselves have a real make-out session with their girlfriend, because they don't want to go too far! So while it may be hard to believe, we have to confront the idea that these thoughts (which aren't usually expressed out loud!) are *normal*. Not *right*, necessarily, but normal. They are going on inside even the nice, trustworthy guys you sit next to in math class.

I think most of us have heard that guys are visual, but have never really understood what that actually *meant*. So in this chapter we'll explore what it means—and what it means for girls. Some of this information is awkward to talk about and hard to hear, but because it is extremely important to understand this part of a guy's nature, we hope you will hang in there as we go.

We need to say right up front that we are not excusing wrong choices. But we all face temptations, and this is one of the main ones for guys. A bit later on, we will talk about the choice that every guy must make, to give in to this temptation or not. But for now, let's define what the temptation itself looks like.

WHAT "GUYS ARE VISUAL" MEANS

Here's the truth:

Even decent guys who are happily "going with" a girl are instinctively pulled to want to visually take in, linger on, and fantasize about all the details of an attractive girl's body. These images can be just as enticing whether they are live or remembered.

Three areas of this "guys are visual" thing surfaced that many of us really don't "get":

1. A girl dressed in any outfit that calls attention to a good figure is an "eye magnet." Any eye magnet is incredibly difficult to avoid, and even if a guy forces himself not to look, he is very much aware of her presence.

2. Even when no eye magnet is present, every guy has a bunch of stored images of other "great bodies" that can pop into his thoughts without warning—or can be called up at will.

3. When a guy sees (or recalls) a girl who is dressed to call attention to her figure, he's strongly tempted to picture her naked—or even naked with him.

If you're among the roughly 25 percent of females who describe themselves as "visual," this may not surprise you. But for the rest of us, it may seem a mystery—or worse. So let's face this directly.

> While it may be hard to believe, we have to confront the idea that these thoughts (which aren't usually expressed out loud!) are *normal*.
> Not necessarily *right*, but normal.

FACT #1: A GUY CAN'T NOT WANT TO LOOK.

SURVEY SAYS:

Imagine you are sitting in class, and a new girl with a great body sits down a few desks over from you. What is your reaction to her?

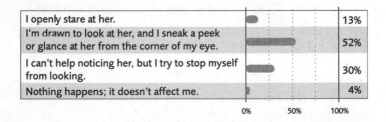

I openly stare at her.	13%
I'm drawn to look at her, and I sneak a peek or glance at her from the corner of my eye.	52%
I can't help noticing her, but I try to stop myself from looking.	30%
Nothing happens; it doesn't affect me.	4%

Almost *all* the guys put their response to an eye-catching girl in "can't *not* be attracted" categories—only 4 percent were unaffected by a girl with a great body. And the results were similar for guys who were currently dating another girl. On the *FWO* survey of adult men, even the happily married men answered the same way.

Many guys explained the power of this desire to look, even when they tried *not* to or when the attractive girl in question left their line of sight. First, look at this comment from a man from *FWO*:

> If I see a woman with a great body walk into Home Depot, even if I close my eyes or turn away until she passes, for the next half hour I'm keenly aware that she's in there somewhere.

Teenagers expressed the same idea. Look at these comments from guys we talked to:

- "When I know there's a hot babe sitting near me in class, a part of my mind will constantly be aware of her."

- "I try to concentrate when I'm at school, but if I'm at the movies or especially at the beach, I'll go ahead and stare, especially if something is popping out."

- "I'm always looking. I'm just wired that way. It has nothing to do with the way I feel about my girl-friend."

Any girl dressed in a way that emphasizes a good figure becomes an eye magnet. And let's be honest: It's *not* her face that the guy is tempted to linger on. In fact, when an eye-magnet girl is present and trying to have a conversation with a guy, guys find her body so distracting that they have to tell themselves to *look at her face, look at her face*. Because that is not where their eyes want to go.

> Any girl dressed in a way that emphasizes a good figure becomes an eye magnet.

So what happens when a guy notices the good body at the next desk—and perhaps even takes in all the details?

FACT #2: A GUY HAS A MENTAL COLLECTION OF SENSUAL IMAGES.

We've all heard that the male half of the population thinks about sex a lot. What we may not have realized was that they aren't exactly *thinking* about sex (as in *planning for it*). Rather, they're *picturing* it, or picturing a sexual image. And many of those pictures are of the girls they know—what that girl looked like in those form-fitting shorts, or that spaghetti-strap top. Also, those images could be those that have been burned in their brains just by living in today's media and culture. And any of these images can arise in their brains at any time, almost like unwanted pop-ups on a computer.

You might be wondering, what kinds of images? Apparently just about anything: the memory of any sexual experiences they may have had—or the memory of the cover of a men's magazine that they caught sight of in the bookstore. It could be a recollection of the hot girl who walked through the parking lot two minutes ago or the porn video a buddy showed him two years ago. These images often arise without warning, even if the guy doesn't want them to. Or specific images can be recalled on purpose. As several guys put it, "I have an unending supply of images in my head."

The Tom Cruise conversation

Now, we might hear about these images popping up in a guy's head and still not understand. I (Shaunti) sure didn't. One day early in my research for *FWO*, my husband Jeff and I were riding in the car, discussing what I was discovering. Jeff was *sure* that I experienced things the same way, and tried to put it in a way that would help me understand:

Jeff: Maybe we are just using different language to describe this. For example, think of a movie star that you find physically attractive—Tom Cruise, say. After we've seen one of his movies, how many times will that attractive image rise up in your mind the next day?

Shaunti: Never.

Jeff: I must not be explaining myself correctly. I mean, how many times will a thought of what he looked like with his shirt off just sort of pop up in your head?

Shaunti: Never.

Jeff: Never—as in never?

Shaunti: Zero times. It just doesn't happen.

Jeff: (After a long pause) Wow.

It's a minefield out there...

For those of us who aren't visual, it's hard to imagine that a guy could have no control over something popping up in his head. We also may not realize that our sex-saturated culture is a minefield of possible triggers and potential images that could be recalled days or years later.

"I have an unending supply of sexual images in my head."

To use a common example, prime-time television commercials often flash sensual two-second images—say, of a woman undressing—that are up on the screen and gone before the guy can look away. Nothing he can do. *Boom*, it's added to the mental collection, whether he wants it to be or not!

And once those thoughts are triggered, the guys told us, an image could rise up several times a minute—and then if they weren't careful they would be tempted to spend "half an hour straight" on it! They explained that if they didn't reject the image immediately, it was even more difficult to get rid of. And that leads us to the next point. Are you ready for the third and most intense reality of a guy's visual nature?

FACT #3: A GUY IS AUTOMATICALLY TEMPTED TO SEXUALLY FANTASIZE ABOUT THE GOOD BODY HE'S SEEN.

As you might have guessed from the discussion above, when a guy sees a hot girl, or her image comes back to mind, he's not necessarily picturing her as he sees her. In fact, unless he's really strict with himself, he is automatically tempted to picture that girl totally naked—and many guys do. And he's tempted to picture her naked with him.

We will refrain from printing here exactly *what* these guys are picturing girls doing with them and to them, but we're sure you can guess. And we hope that you will read the rest of this section carefully.

Honesty on the survey

We asked the young men in our national survey another question, following up on the previous one about the hot girl in class:

> Now imagine that the same hot girl goes to the front of the class to give a report. She's all business, but is wearing clothes that accentuate her figure. If you're not careful, would there be a possibility that you would picture her naked—either now or later?

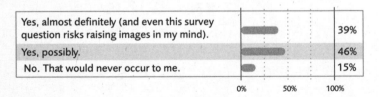

Yes, almost definitely (and even this survey question risks raising images in my mind).	39%
Yes, possibly.	46%
No. That would never occur to me.	15%

0%   50%   100%

In total, 85 percent of guys admit to the possibility of picturing a good-looking girl naked. And it didn't matter whether the guys were old or young, highly educated or high school dropouts, or what ethnic background they were—they all tended to answer the same way. The only real difference was that guys who attended religious services every week were slightly less likely to do this—but at 77 percent of even *those* guys, the number was still the vast majority.

Even a group of teenagers who were leaders in their church's youth department confessed to having these exact same issues. One told us, "When we see a hot girl, the first ten seconds of a guy's thoughts are pretty raw. We go straight into the fantasy mode. And we have to really work to pull things back."

> "When we see a hot girl, our thoughts are pretty raw.... We have to really work to pull things back."

THIS IS NORMAL?

Okay, let's take a deep breath for a second. For some of us, this is a lot to take in. For others, it's no big deal—at least *some* of it isn't. Also, if you are one of the 25 percent of girls who are also "visual," you may more readily understand the typical guy's struggle. And don't worry—you're normal. But it's important for the rest of us to realize that the guys we know and love and trust are normal, too, in having this temptation. Although guys may or may not *act* on it, the national surveys of both adults and teenagers showed that nearly every guy has the temptation itself.

At this point you might be rather alarmed—or even disgusted—that guys are even *tempted* to fantasize about girls' bodies (even if they don't actually do so). But we'd like to point out two things. First, if a girl's clothes choice *doesn't* show off her body, the guy's temptation usually doesn't get triggered! Second, there is another side to this issue, with a positive, logical, God-given root. God *created* guys not just "visual" but with lots of testosterone and a more assertive sex drive—and remember that God said His creation was "good"! Sociologists say that this visual, sexually assertive nature keeps guys invigorated and motivated to pursue the right woman, marry, and have children. Some say that without the high sex drive, men would just have the conquering drive, and they'd stay out hunting or doing battle forever and never develop a deep relationship with a special woman.

As one guy said, "The loveliness and attractiveness of girls causes us to excel—to want to be smarter, faster, and better at everything—all to impress and win the girl. Remember, everything—*everything*—is to impress chicks."

The guys also emphasized, however, that this temptation doesn't magically go away once they do actually "win the girl." It's always there, and has nothing to do with their devotion to or delight in the girl they are with.

It's important for us to realize that the guys we know and love and trust are normal in having this temptation.

THERE IS A DIFFERENCE BETWEEN TEMPTATION AND SIN

To process what we are learning here, let's make a critical distinction between temptation and sin. Remember: The involuntary temptations we face in our life are *not* sins. (The Biblical book of Hebrews states that Jesus was tempted in every way just as we are—yet was without sin.) What we *do* with those temptations is the issue.

We all have temptations in our lives, and because of guys' wiring, one of their main temptations—that they have to fight!—is this desire to constantly "check out" girls. So let's see how this particular temptation "hits" a guy, and what he can and should do about it.

Step 1: For every guy, sensual images and thoughts arrive involuntarily.

Daniel Weiss, the media and sexuality analyst at Focus on the Family, told us, "I would emphasize to women that, yes, men do have these thoughts whether they want them or not."

A high school senior said, "I have a photographic memory for the images of good-looking girls I see. And everything comes back…everything."

In addition, a guy's initial temptation is often not only unintentional, but automatic. If the stimulus is there (a great figure in a tight outfit), so is the response. As one guy put it, "It doesn't even register that I thought *great body* until two seconds later!" Most guys cannot prevent those *initial* thoughts or images from intruding.

Don't believe us? Let us illustrate.

Don't read this.

No really, don't read it. Just look at the letters, and don't read the words.

Impossible, isn't it? There is no way to just notice the letters without reading the word. That's what it's like for a guy. His brain reads "Great body!" without his even realizing it.

One focus group guy—without knowing we were already calling good-looking girls "eye magnets"—compared this situation to being near a magnet:

> I think guys and attractive girls are like positive and negative magnets. As long as the attractive girl is a certain physical distance away, she can remain unnoticed and have no "pull" on him. But once she comes close enough for a guy to actually see her, it's

like she's a strong enough magnet to totally pull his attention. The guy becomes keenly aware of the girl and will continue to be until she leaves the plane again. Keenly aware doesn't necessarily mean jaw-flapping stare, but oh, yeah, we notice that she's *there*.

This actually debunks the popular assumption that all the trouble starts because "men have wandering eyes." A better understanding is that there are wandering women—and men can't not notice them!

> A guy's initial temptation is often not only unintentional, but automatic.

If you're still having a difficult time believing the involuntary nature of this, consider the story of the title character of the biblical book of Job. God describes Job as "the finest man in all the earth—a man of complete integrity." And yet, look at Job's telling statement: "I made a covenant with my eyes not to look with lust upon a young woman."

Why would Job need to take such a step? Surely, the "finest man in all the earth" wouldn't even *have* this struggle, right? Wrong. Job was a man. And all males are prone to this vulnerability, whether we like it or not.

Step 2: Every guy's automatic physical reaction is to enjoy the feelings associated with these thoughts and images.

The reason this temptation is such a struggle for a guy—so difficult to resist—is that the visual images stimulate some powerful feelings inside him. When a sensual image enters a guy's mind (or a great body enters his line of sight), it brings a rush of adrenaline. Speaking bluntly, the guys say it's almost like a short-term rush of sexual pleasure.

One man said, "When an image plays on a man's brain or he gazes at an attractive woman, there's a thrill there. And a man can go back to that adrenaline rush by entertaining those images."

Step 3: But every guy can make a choice— to dwell on the images and thoughts, or to do the work necessary to get rid of them.

This choice is the critical distinction between temptation and sin. Once an image intrudes in a guy's head, he can either linger on it and possibly even start a mental parade, or tear it down immediately and "take every thought captive," as the Bible puts it. A guy can deny himself the pleasure of the image in order to honor God, the girl, or his mental purity—and thus establish deeper pleasure down the road.

Many of the guys we talked to—especially, we noticed,

the guys who regularly attended religious services—seemed to take this choice extremely seriously. They make tough decisions to avoid unwanted visual invitations, to turn away from those that arise, and—when unwanted images arise anyway—to rip them down with all sorts of distractions. We heard that mentally running through baseball scores and car specs were popular thought substitutes!

Here's how one guy put it.

When I see that girl in the short skirt, and I want to stare at her legs—well, okay, I'll be honest, her rear end—I have to *force* myself to look away. Physically wrench my head to looking the other direction, because if I don't, my eyes are going right back. Then, if that image pops up again later that afternoon, I have to go, "Stop it! Don't think about that now!" and tear it down. I'll think about cars, math, sports—whatever it takes to get my thoughts off that body.

Guys also realize this choice is a matter of respecting the girls around them. As one said, "Entertaining the naked image of a girl I know would do injustice to her. I'd like to find out who she is—on the inside."

One church youth group teen said something we

heard from *tons* of guys: "All day long, I have to constantly tell myself not to even open the door. If I do, it's a slippery slope."

Honestly, it sounds exhausting, doesn't it? So, although few guys can stop an involuntary image from popping up in their heads, and few can stop themselves from *wanting* to look, they can (and do) exercise the discipline to stop themselves from actually doing so.

> "All day long, I have to constantly tell myself not to even open the door. If I do, it's a slippery slope."

It is vital that we understand just how much strength and discipline that choice requires. We need to know what our guys are facing every day in this minefield of a culture—and ensure that we aren't making that minefield worse. Which leads us to this question: How can we respond with compassion to this struggle that guys face?

SO WHAT'S A GIRL TO DO?

We're going to ask you to do just three things as you think about the implications of this subject: Put yourself in a guy's shoes, examine your heart, and make any necessary changes.

Put yourself in a guy's shoes

Stop thinking like a girl for a minute and put yourself in a guy's shoes. What must it be like to go through life with this temptation constantly playing in your head—a temptation which could be triggered at any time, even if you don't *want* it ? What must it be like to have to constantly be concerned about dishonoring the girls you know...or worse, dishonoring God?

In one interview, a guy gave us a great example to help girls "get it."

> Girls need to know what they're doing to guys when they tempt them, visually. A girl's equivalent might be how she responds to touch. How would you feel if guys were able to come up and touch you, all day long, whenever they wanted to? How much would you be able to concentrate on school? Well, when you are dressing to emphasize your figure, you are doing that same thing to guys. You're stimulating them visually to the same degree you would be stimulated by constant touch.

After reading *For Women Only*, a schoolteacher sent us an e-mail, telling us how she helped her female high school students understand that this involuntary male temptation really did exist, and what it was like.

To: Shaunti Feldhahn

From:

Subject: what I did with my students

A group of girls came into class upset about
the dress code, saying, "You're a nice
teacher—I'll bet if you were in charge, you
wouldn't have a dress code." I quickly told
them "Oh yes, I would." I tried to explain
the effect of their dress on the guys at the
school, but they immediately attacked the
boys, saying that they were perverts and
shouldn't be looking! That night, God gave me
a great idea for the next day.

For this class, I put the boys in a separate
room. Then I brought out a huge bag of
Hershey's Kisses and put it on the shelf for
all the girls to see. They were very excited
at the possibility of receiving candy. I told
them that they were not to look at the bag
of candy, or else they would have to write
sentences. I told them "Do not even look like
you are looking at the candy, do not talk
about the candy, and by all means do not
even think about touching the candy." I left
to work with the boys, while my poor student
teacher was left to deal with the girls.

When I came back, all the girls had their
folders in front of their faces and many had
received multiple sentences.

I asked, "How many of you had a hard time not looking at the candy? How many of you wanted some candy?" They all raised their hands. I then reminded them of the conversation the previous day. You could see the lightbulbs come on. I told them that by showing off their breasts or rear ends, that was just like saying, "Come have a piece of candy." That is what they put the boys through every day that they show off the wrong things! And I explained that even the nicest boys are going to have to fight not to look.

Yes, even at church...

Although we might wish that the church environment would somehow neutralize a guy's visual temptation, it doesn't. Several guys we interviewed were in worship bands at their churches, and they said the problem with how girls dress in church—and therefore, the temptation—is often just as bad as in a lax school environment. Look at these quotes:

- "It's tough to focus on the worship when there's a girl in a miniskirt on the third row. I have to close my eyes to keep from getting distracted. People think I'm worshiping when I'm actually having a major internal struggle."

- "As far as leading worship goes, girls are definitely a distraction. The only remedy I know of is to close your eyes. The pastor of one church actually had to make a girl move because of how she was dressed. He said, 'Someone get this girl out of the front row.'"

> "Even the nicest boys are going to have to fight not to look."

"'Cute' is not in my vocabulary..."

One of the main problems for most girls is that they simply don't realize what clothes choices stimulate a guy in the wrong way. Many girls think an outfit is "cute"—when that is *not* what the guys are thinking at all.

Several guys in our focus group told us stories about how they would be walking down the hall at school and see a good-looking girl in a tight outfit that looked incredibly hot, which sent their brain spinning onto a track that they really didn't want to be on. Then a moment later, another girl would come up to the first girl and say something like, "What a cute outfit!" As one guy told us, rather shocked, "How can a girl think *that* is *cute*??"

Another guy agreed that, "In that instance, 'cute' is not in my vocabulary."

Many girls think an outfit is "cute"—when that is not what the guys are thinking at all.

Guys think girls know exactly what they are doing

We may not understand what we are doing to the guys around us—but guys find that almost impossible to believe. Nearly every single guy we asked said something like, "Oh, they know exactly what they are doing to us." In other words—if you dress in a tight or revealing outfit, they think you *want* them to picture you naked.

If you are like many other teenage girls, you may have known that a guy was checking you out if you dressed a certain way...but since you probably didn't understand what was actually going on in his brain, you may not have minded. You probably even welcomed the attention! But once girls see the statistics on how often those clothes tempt a guy to picture them naked, they usually become uncomfortable. Here's how Lisa's daughter Sarah put it:

> I should have known this because guys joke about it all the time. They say things like, "Hey baby, I'd like to see you without that sweater on. It leaves too much to my imagination." But even though guys

look and guys joke, girls don't let themselves think too deeply about it. Honestly, I would guess that about 20 percent of girls at my school know that guys are picturing them naked. And even they are probably mostly dressing that way not *because* it sends a guy's brain to a bad place, but because it feels good to get that attention—even if they sub-consciously know it's the wrong kind of attention. It's their moment on the stage, and it feels good.

> If you dress in a tight or revealing outfit, they think you *want* them to picture you naked.

Examine your own heart

Now that you've put yourself in a guy's shoes, take a look at yourself. How do you feel about all of this? Are you interested, perhaps a little convicted, and willing to do your part? Or are you skeptical, not believing it? Or even a bit angry, and resent-ful? Are you finding yourself saying, "It's his problem—no way should I have to change just because some guys can't keep their eyes to themselves!"

I (Lisa) must confess that I have blown it in this area. I remember (*way* back) when I was a young teen. A guy at church came up to me and asked, "What would you say if someone told you that the skirts you wear are too short and are causing some of the guys to struggle with lust?" In my immaturity I answered, "I'd say it was no one's business what I wear."

I look back on that now and think, *God, forgive me!* This poor guy had the boldness to speak to me about an important issue, and I was too blind and immature to hear it, or make any personal changes. Girls, please learn from my stupidity! Please let my painful memory count for something!

If you ever find yourself thinking, *It's no one's business what I wear*, or, *It's the guys' problem and they just have to get over it*, please realize that what you are actually saying is, *I want to do what I like, even if it hurts someone else.*

We believe that most of you would never truly want to hurt the guys around you. If you now realize that that is what you have been doing, please confess that to God, ask for forgiveness, and resolve instead to honor the guys you know.

Are you interested, perhaps a little convicted, and willing to do your part?

See dress codes as a blessing

As your eyes are opened on these issues, you may actually appreciate certain restrictions—like school dress codes or parental "hassles" over clothes—that may have annoyed you before. Many of us used to think of "modesty" standards as being old-fashioned rules designed to perhaps protect us, but certainly to spoil our fun—when now you know they are designed to protect the *guys* even more.

And once we understand just how quickly a certain type of outfit could trigger certain thoughts in a guy's mind, most girls *want* to stay safely on the right side of that line! Which brings us to the next point.

Make any necessary changes

Let's face it: Girls who are clueless about this problem are also contributing to it. After all, the images in a guy's mental collection come from *somewhere*—and it's not just from pictures. The eye magnets on the street are choosing to dress the way they do. But as you know, it's not that easy to dress modestly these days and still feel like you look great—unless it's the middle of winter. The stores that you probably like the best carry tight, revealing choices—or extra-baggy pants that are unflattering.

Lots of girls have told us that they want to dress modestly, but have trouble finding clothes that still make them look good. Several girls admitted, though, that any smart teen *can* find creative ways to look both modest and attractive. As one put it, "We know what to do if we want to do it. We can put that extra layer on, or avoid wearing that short short miniskirt…make little changes. We still want to look pretty, but girls know 'pretty' versus 'slutty,' and unless you've been raised in the desert by wolves, you understand this."

This area is so important that we did a little extra research to find you more practical help and wisdom in the area of modesty. We spoke with Vicki Courtney, author of books and articles dealing with the top issues girls face, including her online magazine, virtuousreality.com. Her organization also offers a girls' "Yada Yada" event that is both educational and entertaining. It includes a fashion show featuring clothes that are flattering *and* modest.

ASK THE EXPERT: Vicki Courtney, author of *TeenVirtue: A Teen Girl's Survival Guide* and Editor-in-Chief, virtuousreality.com

Practical tips for looking great, without the lure

Your clothing is like a label. It tells the world what's on the inside. The problem is that some labels give the wrong message about a girl. They can misrepresent who you really are.

For instance, we asked some teen boys to comment

on different girls walking by at a mall. One girl walked by wearing a little shirt that showed her belly, and the guys said, "Now there's an invitation. She's saying, 'Come and get it.'"

Did the girl really mean, "Come and get it?" Or was she just trying to look cute and trendy for a day at the mall? We've got to look at what message our label is sending. And you can look cute and trendy without the wrong message!

The fashion shows offered at our Yada Yada events display hot new outfits from all the major teen magazines. Then, a live model walks out in a similar outfit that's been modified to make it less revealing. Some ideas:

- Many of the shirts today are small enough to fit my five-pound Yorkie. As long as they are not too tight across your bust, some shirts can be "modest-fied" by adding a cute camisole underneath that overlaps the waistband of your jeans.

- Shirts with spaghetti straps can easily be covered with a cute jacket or hoodie. Exposed bra straps are tacky, tacky, tacky—and cause guys to struggle.

- Be careful of low, plunging necklines where you can see cleavage. Trust me, it will be hard to get a guy to look you in the eye respectfully if you give him a second choice!

- Stay away from jeans that are so tight that you can see the date of a dime in your back pocket.

- Low-rise jeans are not a problem as long as you wear longer shirts or cami's that cover up the waistband. A good rule of thumb is to raise your hands above your head to see if your shirt creeps up to expose your midriff. And make sure you aren't flashing skin from behind when you're sitting down.

- Steer clear of micro minis and short shorts. If you drop something on the ground, you may as well leave it there because it's near impossible to pick it up without making a scene!

Do a "closet check" and a "mirror check," and ask yourself whether each outfit says "pure" or "lure." In other words, am I giving off a message that I'm pure, or one that says I'm trying to lure the guys in?

Once you know how guys view you and what message you're giving off, the Holy Spirit will convict you on a case by case basis about your choices. Yes, you have to shop harder and longer to make modest choices, but when you do, you'll find that your self-worth rises...and you'll get the right kind of attention from the right kind of people.

Remember, one day, you'll probably get married, and that means your future husband is sitting in class somewhere, trying to fight off the distractions that other girls' tight clothing is causing him. And the guy sitting next to you—who might be having problems over what you're wearing—will be married to someone else in a few years.

Again, let's follow the Golden Rule, which is basically "Do unto others as you would have them do unto you." Treat the guys you know like you would want the girls in your future husband's class to treat him! And we know that God will see to it that every good choice you make bears fruit. He'll always reward a heart that wants to do right.

In the next chapter, we'll look at a completely different consequence of the fact that guys are visual. But for now, we'll leave you with a quote from one college guy we interviewed: "Besides 'wear sunscreen' and 'tip well,' my advice to teen girls is, 'understand your identity.' You are a valuable creation of God with an awesome future ahead of you. Understand where you're going, or you'll always be looking for guys to make you content. Quit buying into the lies of the media on how to dress and act, and don't be afraid to stand apart from the crowd."

Chapter 6

SEEING THE INNER AND OUTER BEAUTY

Why Guys Care That Girls Take Care of Themselves—Even Though They Are Looking for the Real You

Guys are attracted to girls with good personalities, as well as inner and outer beauty and confidence. They want a real girl, not a perfect Barbie doll. But they can't force themselves to be attracted to someone.

Please read this chapter prayerfully.

In the movie *Shallow Hal*, Hal is a party boy who chases beautiful babes and strings of meaningless relationships. He suddenly finds himself under a hypnotic spell that makes him see only the inner beauty of the ladies he meets. Now, most of the sexy party gals are not attractive to him. He finds himself going for girls that are kind, sweet, loving, giving, and unselfish, even if they are homely or fat. In the end he drives off into the sunset with a severely obese girl because he's fallen in love with her heart.

In our focus groups, we asked the guys whether this movie was realistic at all—especially its loud message that "it's all about the heart."

What we heard was, interestingly, that it *is* about the heart—but not *all* about it.

It turns out that guys are much more interested in finding a real girl with a great personality than with finding a girl who is beautiful to look at but unpleasant to be with. That said, however, as much as guys want to be "heart-minded," their visual nature won't let them be attracted *solely* to a girl's heart. In order to want a dating relationship, they have to be attracted to a girl's physical appearance as well. As we said in the previous chapter, this doesn't mean wearing the skin-tight clothes that cause the guy to struggle. It *does* mean that he sees you as someone who takes care of herself.

> As much as guys want to be "heart-minded," their visual nature won't let them be attracted *solely* to a girl's heart.

In fact, guys see the effort a girl makes to take care of herself physically as a primary signal of how she *feels about herself* emotionally. For example, either skin-tight clothes *or* being quite overweight often convey to a guy that a girl is insecure in who she is. And that makes all the difference in whether she falls into the category of "just friends" or potential girlfriend. A guy simply can't imagine driving off into the sunset with a girl who just doesn't feel very good about herself.

We'll explore this a bit more deeply in a minute. But first, we need to look you in the eye (so to speak) and make sure you fully hear what we're *not* saying.

A few things we're *not* saying

Because we're talking here about girls' weight and other aspects of physical appearance, we debated long and hard about whether to even *write* this chapter. Nearly all females have some form of body insecurity that we already worry way too much about. We are hammered relentlessly by media messages that we should all look like Jessica Alba (in her skintight *Fantastic Four* bodysuit no less!), and we worry that guys won't be interested if we don't. (Which, as we will show you, is completely untrue.)

But when this chapter *does* talk about ways we can take better care of ourselves, we need you to hear us on this: We are *only* dealing with weight, fitness, and appearance issues that we can *healthfully* do something about.

Let us say that again: *Everything we say in this chapter*—every quote from a guy, every recommendation we make—is consistent *only* with those weight, fitness, and appearance issues that girls can address in a *healthy* manner. If you find yourself tempted to starve yourself, purge, or do anything else unhealthy, you've completely misunderstood us—and we encourage you to talk to a wise and trusted adult about it right away.

> We are only dealing with weight, fitness, and appearance issues that we can healthfully do something about.

A bit later in the chapter, we'll discuss some healthy and unhealthy approaches to this topic. I (Lisa) will share my own story of how I struggled with a distorted body image and a devastating eating disorder. We'll also get an expert's take on it. But first, let's hear what the guys have to say.

WHAT MATTERS TO A GUY— AND WHAT DOESN'T

We heard five truths from teen guys about what matters to them—and what doesn't.

First, and most encouragingly, we were a bit surprised that

the guys themselves demolished the suspicion of many females, that guys will only go for the perfect, gorgeous babes.

Fact #1: Guys like (and will fall for) all types of girls.

Do guys really fall for girls who are strong on personality but short on looks? Or do guys secretly just want the cover girl?

SURVEY SAYS:

TV and magazines glamorize a particular kind of girl that everyone seems to agree is hot. Despite this image, do you find yourself attracted to other kinds of girls, such as any of the following?

• the pretty but unglamorous "girl next door"

• the "plain Jane" who is a fantastic athlete

• the sweet girl that never made an enemy

• the stocky girl with a hilarious sense of humor

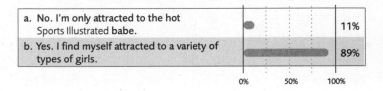

a. No. I'm only attracted to the hot Sports Illustrated **babe**.	11%
b. Yes. I find myself attracted to a variety of types of girls.	89%

0%   50%   100%

Nine out of ten guys say they are attracted to all different types of girls! Only a small minority insists upon the *Sports*

Illustrated babe with the perfect body. And that number almost vanished among Christian guys who regularly attend church. Nearly 100 percent of those guys confirmed that they want real girls, in the real world.

This was exactly what we had been hearing in the guy-on-the-street interviews.

Over and over again, we heard each guy say that they weren't going for a girl who looked like a television or movie star. As a matter of fact, most of the focus groups spoke strongly *against* girls feeling like they had to achieve such a goal. Guys know how hard girls are on themselves, and that they just don't need to be.

One guy put it really well: "Girls should throw away their magazines and turn off the TV. It's unrealistic, and that's not what real guys want."

Another one said, "For me, the really skinny chick is a downer. It's unnatural. I don't want a girl I can break."

Another guy said, "I don't know why girls don't seem to believe us on this. Guys aren't looking for the perfect fakey bikini babe. We *like* the individual, real-life girl."

Consistently, the guys told us that they don't notice or care about the less-than-ideal proportions or particular features that we get so obsessed about. In fact, most guys said over and over that they wished normal, average, healthy girls would quit being so oversensitive about their bodies!

There were many things beyond the stereotypical "great body" that guys found attractive.

A girl with personality and smarts is attractive

Most guys told us that they really enjoy and are attracted to girls that can carry on witty conversations with them. And most wouldn't take a "hot" girl who had turned off her brain and personality. Listen to this comment: "There are some insanely attractive girls that are sickeningly dumb. Beyond just taking care of herself, the girl really does have to have knowledge and personality. Intelligent conversation is a good thing."

The sweet "girl next door" is attractive

Guys also repeatedly said that they want to date the "girl next door"—the girl who is sweet, approachable, and shows a balance of inner and outer beauty.

- "An average girl is more beautiful, I think. She's more real, and accessible. I can't explain it, but it's like 'the girl next door' is someone I can have a conversation with…versus an untouchable debutante."

- "If I'm looking at a 'hot' girl, I'm never wondering if she'd want to play basketball with me. But the 'girl next door' would, and that's who I want to spend time with."

- "Modesty is attractive. That girl is a mystery, and that's attractive."

- "I want someone modest, innocent, good."

- "I'm attracted to a real girl…One with humor, who laughs a lot and is easy to be around."

The godly girl is attractive

There were many guys in our focus groups—and from the national survey—who expressed their desire to have a godly girlfriend. Here are some of their comments:

- "Seeing a passionate love for God is so attractive."

- "I want to date a girl who's on my level, spiritually, who's heading the same direction."

- "Sometimes I look at a girl and try to picture her doing the things I dream about doing some day…like spending time on the mission field, working in an orphanage. If I can't picture it, I'm not going to date her."

There is a reason the Bible talks about having the "beauty" of a quiet and gentle spirit. That sort of spirit is actually *attractive* to guys.

"Modesty is attractive. That girl is a mystery, and that's attractive."

Fact #2: Physical attraction is necessary for a dating relationship.

Now, all of that said, almost every guy we interviewed *also* emphasized that there had to be physical attraction in order for them to be interested in dating a girl—even if they were not intending to get physically involved before marriage. Physical attraction was not *the* most important value, they said, but it had to be there in order for them to think about a girl as a potential date, not just a good friend.

As one guy said, "We have to be attracted to how she looks, to pursue something with a girl. Even if she has a great personality, if she's not really taking care of herself, she's just going to be that good friend. You have to be physically attracted if you want a relationship."

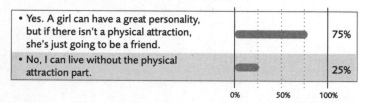

While there may be multiple factors that would attract you to a girl in a romantic way, is physical attraction essential for a meaningful, lasting relationship?

• Yes. A girl can have a great personality, but if there isn't a physical attraction, she's just going to be a friend.		75%
• No, I can live without the physical attraction part.		25%

0%   50%   100%

There are many girls reading this book that might be encouraged that 25 percent of the surveyed guys said physical attraction *wasn't* a must in a relationship. However, we also noticed that the older the guys got, the more likely they were to say that physical attraction was important. So let's deal with the feelings of the majority, and the primary "physical attraction" point they referenced.

> "We have to be attracted to how she looks, to pursue something with a girl."

They wanted girls to be a healthy weight

Not surprisingly, of all the physical attraction issues guys spoke about, a girl's weight was what they mentioned most often. For most of the guys, a significant weight gain acted like a "blocker" that simply blocked out the ability to be physically attracted to the girl—no matter how wonderful and beautiful she otherwise was. To them it said that she didn't feel particularly good about herself—a fact we will deal with in a moment.

As one guy admitted, "I'd have a hard time dating a fat girl. I know it sounds shallow, but it's the truth." Another, listening, agreed: "You need to be healthy."

One teenager gave us an example, saying,

Um, there's a girl in my youth group who would otherwise be attractive, but she's a little heavy and she wears those shirts that are in style now that are just a little too short to reach the top of her jeans. But since she's a bit overweight it would be much more attractive if she was covered up and didn't have that fat thing coming out of the middle. I see that all the time these days, and it's a real turn-off.

We have to admit that there were some amusing exceptions to this rule, however. One high school guy admitted that he loves big girls.

"I must admit I like fat women. Not fat and ugly, of course, but if they're fat and beautiful, bring them on! As a matter of fact, you tell those big, beautiful women to call me! My name is Michael Cooke...that's Cooke with an e... My number is 463..."

Why can't guys just be "spiritually minded"?

The "Michael Cooke's" of the world aside, many women are bothered by the high value that most guys put on appearance, thinking it shouldn't matter. FWO also included a chapter on making an effort toward appearance, and in an email one woman said how disappointed she was by it. She said that she knew she was significantly overweight, but added, "Please pray for me, that I would find a man who is spiritually minded and not so interested in outward things."

This email saddened us because this lady clearly didn't get it. She wrongly believed that if a guy is spiritual, he wouldn't be focusing on the five senses. Our research—and that of others—proves that this wishful thinking just doesn't bear out in reality. In truth, guys are designed by God to be attracted to both inner *and* outer beauty.

While the general culture emphasizes physical appeal *too* much, somehow the church seems to have gone too far in the other direction. Among Christians it has become a bit taboo to speak frankly about the importance of physical attraction. "God looks not on the outward appearance, but on the heart," we say, and expect our guys to do the same.

Or because we know "it's what's inside that counts," we can easily migrate to the idea that what's outside doesn't matter.

But what's on the outside *does* matter. And when we seem to be willfully ignoring that truth, guys assume that we are doing so because we just don't think very highly of ourselves. And that is just not attractive to them.

Guys are designed by God to be attracted to both inner and outer beauty.

Fact #3: Your effort changes everything.

Just as guys are attracted to different types of girls, they are also able to *become* attracted to girl who is willing to *make the effort to take care of herself*. Whether that means little things like dressing neatly or keeping hair brushed, or bigger things like eating healthfully and getting fit, those efforts can completely change how a guy views a girl.

SURVEY SAYS:

Suppose you knew a girl with a great personality, whom you had not previously been attracted to because she was a bit overweight and didn't seem to care about her appearance. If you saw that girl making a real effort to eat right and get in shape, could you become attracted to her down the road?

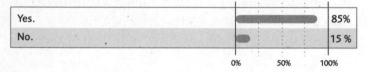

Yes.		85%
No.		15 %

0%   50%   100%

Here's what some of the guys said:

- "If she did work out, put on some makeup, tried to look more attractive, it would be different. It could work then."

- "I know a girl that, if she just tried a little harder, and maybe had some help from her girlfriends, she would be really attractive."

- "I help my girlfriend work out, and we keep each other on track. We're both making the effort for each other. Because it matters."

- "The effort to look nice goes a long way, but there is a balance. I'd rather spend the time with my girlfriend than enjoy the results of the two hours she spent fixing her hair. But that said, yes, it really is nice to see she's put some effort in for me."

Okay, so these "visual" guys make the connection and appreciate the effort we put into our appearance.

But they do wish that some girls would make the connection, too. So many guys told us that they knew many girls—great, funny, terrific girls—who never seem to get a boyfriend, and don't see a connection between that and the fact that they are twenty or thirty pounds over a healthy weight.

Guys make the connection and appreciate the effort we put into our appearance.

We assume that there are probably at least some girls reading this book whose doctors might have said, for example, that they are overweight and need to take better care of themselves. So what kind of effort is healthy and appropriate, and what kind of effort does more harm than good? This is probably a great time to share my (Lisa's) own story of a horrible struggle with a distorted body image and a life-wrecking eating disorder.

Walking a thin line

When I was in high school, like many girls, I was very self-conscious about my body. Even though I was well proportioned, I was taller than the rest of my friends. And I had hips! I was always envious of my more petite friends.

To make matters worse, I had several family members who were significantly overweight and not getting any better, despite constant dieting. This *terrified* me, and I vowed to find a way to conquer what seemed like a devastating genetic curse. Unfortunately, the way I found threw me into a dark season of secrecy, shame, dysfunction, and despair.

A friend told me how if she wanted to eat something fattening, she would simply taste a bite of it and then quickly spit it into the trash. That way, she could enjoy a moment of some yummy "forbidden" food without it landing on her hips. It was a terrific plan, I thought, and I followed her example. There were constantly little chunks of half-chewed food pieces in the trash, though I tried hiding them or flushing them whenever possible.

The problem got worse when I went off to a university that promoted the perfect balance of "mind, spirit, and body." Since little was understood at the time about how easily eating disorders can start, the school made it clear that we were to look good as examples of Christians with every area of our lives under control. Lots of female students were into full-fledged bulimia (bingeing on rich foods, then purging by vomiting, or taking laxatives), and I unfortunately joined right in. The sad thing is that no matter how we looked on the outside, on the inside we were totally messed up—and afraid to talk about it.

What kind of effort is healthy and appropriate, and what kind of effort does more harm than good?

Not until after college did I get some real help. Through counseling, reading good books on the subject, lots of prayer, and the grace of God, I overcame the anguish of bulimia. Now, I am a normal weight, and I have very healthy guidelines that I follow for eating. I generally follow a lower-carb eating plan because foods high in carbohydrates and sugars (breads, donuts, desserts, etc.) can trigger my old bulimic ways. The higher protein/lower carb plans tend to even out my blood sugar and keep me from having cravings. I usually let myself have a certain number of carbs a day, and that seems to be the easiest form of accountability for me. A free Internet program called www.fitday.com has also helped me maintain good eating habits.

But remember: Everyone is different. For her part, Shaunti has kept off the weight she lost by following the principles and education she got from reading *The South*

Beach Diet, and its terrific balance and inclusion of "good carbs" and "good fats." The key is to set a goal and address it in a consistent and healthy way, for life.

By contrast, I found out the hard way that my short-term, unhealthy solution of bulimia not only causes all sorts of medical problems—it actually messes with your body so much that it makes it *harder* to lose weight in the end.

If you think you might have a tendency toward an eating disorder, please don't live in secrecy and shame—and actually *mess up* your ability to stay a healthy weight! Please talk to a trusted counselor or medical professional and get some help.

Remember, God *will* help you with this. He made you, after all, and He wants good things for your life. He wants to set you free from any destructive worries in this area.

Fact #4: Your appearance sends a signal of how you feel about yourself.

As we mentioned earlier, one of the main reasons most guys said they wouldn't be attracted to a significantly overweight girl was simply because it signaled that she didn't care much about herself. As the guys see it, they want girls that think enough of themselves to put effort into their appearance. That showed the guys that the girl was confident in who she was as a person.

That sense of confidence is one main reason why the

guys said over and over that they could go for different types of girls. It didn't matter so much if the girl looked like a movie star, model, or was a bit stocky or gangly: When her confidence in herself shone through, it was truly attractive to him.

Over and over we heard almost this same exact sentence from a lot of teenage guys we interviewed: *"If she likes who she is, it's attractive."*

> "If she likes who
> she is, it's attractive."

Look at these other, similar comments:

- "It's very attractive if a girl is confident…if she knows who she is and what she wants."

- "A lot of girls feel they have to be perfect, but that comes from insecurity. I want a girl who feels secure in herself."

Let's investigate this just a bit more by asking another expert for her opinion on this. Dr. Linda Mintle is a psychotherapist who works with women and girls on body-image issues, and has authored multiple books, including one book on how to get in shape (*Lose It for Life*) and another book on making peace with yourself and accepting your body no matter how you look (*Making Peace with Your Thighs*). We asked her what she would say to teen girls on this issue of making an effort with their appearance, and what guys think about it.

ASK THE EXPERT: Dr. Linda Mintle, Body-image Psychotherapist and author of *Overweight Kids*

Weight doesn't define you

The reality is that weight and appearance can initially be either a turn-on or a turn-off to boys. If a girl is not at a healthy weight, she can understand a guy's reaction by asking herself this question: If I don't have enough respect for myself to want to take care of my body, why would a guy be eager to pursue knowing me better? Our outward appearance can be a reflection of what's inside our hearts. One message we give when we are not at a healthy weight is "I don't care about myself." And that is not attractive to people.

However, girls also should not say, "I need to lose weight to please this guy." That's a dangerous road. Because then your identity becomes all about that other person, and that is not healthy either! You don't want to always be dependent on others for approval. Instead, focus on who you are, and who God wants you to be. Getting healthy should be motivated by wanting to take care of your body as the temple of the Holy Spirit, and giving the message that you respect yourself, regardless of the opinions of others. That confidence will be attractive.

Now, research shows that when most females look in mirrors, we all think we need to lose weight—even girls who don't. So if you think you need to lose weight, what I suggest is to ask a trusted adult woman who can take you aside and give you an honest assessment. Because if you do want to change something, you first need to make sure that change is really necessary. Then, enlist a trusted person's help in approaching change in a healthy way. Healthy weight loss usually involves changing bad habits like eating junk foods, downing sodas, and munching on sugary snacks. Don't eat out of boredom or when you are upset. Learn other ways to cope with stress. And teenage girls are the worst when it comes to exercise, so get active.

Talking about weight is a sensitive topic because on the one hand we have too many girls obsessing and developing eating disorders and engaging in dangerous dieting, and on the other hand, we have record rates of teen obesity. So dealing with your weight in a healthy way is important. If a trusted woman confirms that your weight is a good issue to work on, use this information as a wake-up call to get healthy and take care of yourself. Do this out of self-respect. Realizing that as you respect yourself more, the more attractive you will be to other people.

Remember, no matter your weight, your identity includes more than your physical appearance. Worth should not be tied to weight! Your true worth comes from being a child of God. And that fact never changes with your weight!

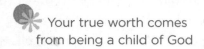

Your true worth comes from being a child of God

Fact #5: Guys want to find a genuine "diamond in the rough."

Many guys that we interviewed talked about wanting to find a "diamond in the rough": a unique and genuine girl who has tons of potential to be a beauty in the future, even if she is going through a rough or awkward stage right now. Here's what some of the guys said:

- "A lot of girls in middle and young high school go through an awkward stage with so many changes.

But smart guys can tell who the diamond in the rough will be, and they'll look past the awkwardness of the moment."

- "We like to feel we can spot the 'diamond in the rough' and go for girls with great potential."

Perhaps because of this, lots of the guys said that they had a big problem with fakeness in girls. They hate it! And they told us they even felt that way about the "hot" girls who dressed in really tight or revealing clothes. They want the real girl—the real diamond that really is in there—not someone who feels like they have to camouflage who they really are. Here's what some of them had to say:

- "Girls who are 'over the top' are out. Too much makeup, fake tan, fake nails, and fake hair is a turnoff. Makes me think they're hung up on themselves and wouldn't give the relationship a chance."

- "If you have to be sleazy to get a guy, that guy is not worth it. If you have to make yourself something you're not, that's not something worth going after. Some girls spend all their time trying to be attractive, and playing with a guy's heart and mind. They use their charms to pull you in, then push you away."

- "I like the ones without a ton of makeup...just classy."

- "Putting on a lot of makeup will attract the wrong kind of guy. You'll fall in love with someone who doesn't love you for you."

"We like to feel we can spot the 'diamond in the rough' and go for girls with great potential."

WHERE DO I START?

We hope you see that the guys you care about truly do care about you, the real girl, and enjoy your individuality. Even if this chapter has opened your eyes to things you might want to work on, we urge you to do so in a careful way that honors the special person God created *you* to be. If you have decided to take some steps to build a more healthy you, here's how you might lay a good foundation:

Enlist that trusted friend

As our expert Dr. Mintle suggested, enlist a trusted adult woman to help you with a realistic assessment of your overall fitness and appearance. Or even consider asking a trusted, close, reliable girlfriend—but only if you are sure she will have your best interests at heart. My (Lisa's) daughter Sarah cautions, "Don't ask the girls who ridicule you when your belt doesn't perfectly match your shirt! Find a true friend and get a real answer." And for the sake of your sanity, remember the words *realistic* and *overall*. This doesn't apply to someone who is fit and trim but thinks she needs to lose five pounds, or is just dissatisfied with certain features of her body.

We strongly suggest that you *not* ask this of your father or a guy friend. Dads love their little girls no matter what, and know that a word about weight or appearance can create real emotional turmoil. Younger guys will usually just clam up if a girl asks about it, because it's just too uncomfortable to talk about. They also don't want to hurt her feelings. They just know, as one guy told us, "Nothing good can come from having that conversation!"

Follow a reasonable plan that you can stick with for the long term

As we mentioned, both of us have learned that taking weight off and keeping it off is very do-able. But taking care of yourself requires making a purposeful effort to eat right and live a healthy lifestyle over the long term. Most of us need a long-term plan we can stick with, that is not too "boot camp-ish," but is still effective.

Thankfully, there are many resources available to help you these days. We list some at the website www.foryoungwomenonly.com.

Realize God cares and He will help you!

This might sound funny, but it's true: God really will help you address this health and fitness issue in amazing ways, if you realize you need to.

God didn't create us to be Barbie dolls. So let's celebrate our God-given individuality and body—sturdy thighs, small boobs, and all—and make the best of them.

> So let's celebrate our God-given individuality and body and make the best of them!

God will bless your desire to show on the outside the self-respect you feel on the inside. Remember, He says our bodies are the "temple of the Holy Spirit" (I Corinthians 6:19). So if you ask Him for help and are committed to implementing it, we truly believe He will give you a *permanent* internal motivation to have a healthy "temple."

I hope you have considered the message of this chapter prayerfully, allowing God to give you peace, rather than a knot in your stomach. He is a God of peace, after all. And He loves us no matter what our imperfections are.

Chapter 7

BODY
LANGUAGE

His Physical Desires = Emotional
Consequences for Both of You

*Teenage guys are conflicted by their powerful
physical urges, which also have massive
emotional consequences, and they need you
to help protect both of you.*

In the book and movie *The Sisterhood of the Traveling Pants*, four best friends who spend their summer vacations in different places decide to share a mysterious pair of jeans that somehow fit each of them. The girls make a pact to mail these jeans from one to another throughout the summer, along with a letter describing their adventures while they have them.

Most of the adventures, of course, revolve around guys. While some of the girls make wise decisions, others make very poor ones. Bridget, the beautiful, blond seventeen-year-old athlete goes off to Mexico for summer camp, glad to get away from her job-centered dad who ignores her. She decides that capturing the attention and affection of the handsome college-age soccer coach is the only thing that will soothe her aching heart, and she spends all her spare time coming up with interesting ways to seduce him.

The young soccer coach is both thrilled and nervous that Bridget is trying to seduce him. Everything in him wants the pleasure she's strongly hinting can be his, and it scares and excites him to see where the relationship might be heading. But when he actually gives in, Bridget ends up depressed instead of delighted. She tells her friends that sex left her feeling incomplete rather than healed, saying, "How can something that is supposed to make you feel complete make you feel so empty?"

And although viewers might assume the handsome young man was just glad to get a little action with no emotional ties, that is not what happens. The coach is left sad, disillusioned, and loaded with some weighty baggage he'll have to carry into his future. This was not what he was anticipating when he decided to get together with this beautiful girl.

HIS EMOTIONAL SIDE

In this chapter we're going to examine several unseen dynamics that go on inside a guy's heart and mind after having a sexual encounter. Girls often don't know these exist, but they powerfully affect a guy—and therefore they powerfully affect you. Here's a quick summary:

- Many guys don't feel the ability or the responsibility to stop the sexual progression with you. And those who *do* feel the responsibility don't want to have to stop it alone.

- In a guy's mind, sex doesn't equal love and/or commitment to you.

- As soon as you have sex with a guy, he'll likely doubt whether he can trust you from then on.

- Guys really want to marry a virgin.

Let's take these findings one at a time.

Emotional Fact #1: Many guys feel neither the ability nor the responsibility to stop the sexual progression with you. And those who *do* feel the responsibility don't want to have to stop it alone.

Many guys admitted that they doubt both their a) ability and b) responsibility to stop sexual activity once it's started. The national survey confirmed this.

SURVEY SAYS:

Whether or not you are currently involved with a girl-friend, if you were to be in a make-out situation with a willing partner who does not signal a desire to stop, how do you feel about your ability to stop the sexual progression?

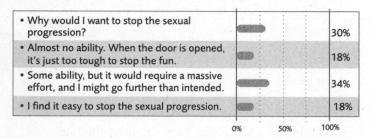

• Why would I want to stop the sexual progression?	30%
• Almost no ability. When the door is opened, it's just too tough to stop the fun.	18%
• Some ability, but it would require a massive effort, and I might go further than intended.	34%
• I find it easy to stop the sexual progression.	18%

0%   50%   100%

Little ability...

That adds up to 82 percent of guys reporting serious difficulty in bringing things to a halt in a make-out situation—or no desire to halt things at all! For a guy even more than a girl, making out often starts a physical drive toward sex that requires a *major* effort to override.

As one high school junior said, "With basic making out, it's usually innocent for me. But once the hands start moving, it leads to more stuff. I can usually restrain myself if the girl isn't pushing things too much, but if she is…"

Another guy said, "With a guy, if you want to be able to stop it, it's safest to not even start."

> "With a guy, if you want to be able to stop it, it's safest to not even start."

Because of the extreme effort involved in stopping, it's not surprising that even the nicest guys come up with all sorts of ways to rationalize *not* stopping. Look at the excuse one high school senior came up with: "The problem is that if I stop the sexual progression, the girl might think, 'Wow, am I not good enough for him?'"

Little responsibility...

Not only do guys feel that it's physically very difficult to stop, a sizeable minority feel almost no responsibility to stop.

On the previous survey question, almost one-third answered, "Why would I want to stop the sexual progression?" In other words: "I'm not going to. It's her responsibility, not mine!"

A *lot* of the guys we interviewed echoed that point, saying that unless the girl protested, they had no qualms about "going all the way."

As one high schooler bluntly put it, shrugging, "Where we stop is totally up to her." Look at these comments:

- "Girls are the ones that set the limits. For guys, there are no limits. We'll go all the way."

- "Yes, I confess, in the physical realm, I'll keep going till the choo-choo train has expired."

- "I look to the girl to let me know how far we should take things. If it were up to me, we'd go all the way."

On the survey, the percentage that felt no responsibility was even higher (38 percent) among wealthier guys, and among those who described themselves as having no particular religious beliefs. And it was a bit lower (23 percent) among Christian guys who attended church once a week.

One high school senior said, "It's easier to stop if you're going out with the girl, because your conscience is asking you how this is going to affect your relationship. But if you're in a casual relationship, it doesn't matter."

"Where we stop is totally up to her."

They don't want to be the only "strong" one

A lot of the responsible guys we talked to didn't want to have to be the *only* one trying to stop. They wanted and even *needed* the girl's help, so they didn't have to be the only "strong" one. When they were thinking clearly, they actively *wanted* girls to be more cautious. And this was echoed by *many* of the guys on the survey.

As the final question on the survey, we gave the guys a blank space and asked what their top advice would be for girls in life, including their little sister. It's probably no surprise that most answers dealt with sex in some way! What *was* a surprise was the large number of guys who said things like, "Be careful," "Be cautious," "Watch out." This was one of the strongest themes that emerged on the whole survey. In fact, one out of every five guys chose to use the blank space to focus only on that.

One survey-taker touched on this issue of a guy's ability— or responsibility—to stop:

"Guys are only looking for one thing. Make sure you know what kind of guy you have, and be very careful. I can stop you if I want to—but you need to make sure *you take care of yourself.*"

Christian guys

In our interviews we did see a difference in a couple key areas between guys who identified themselves as Christians who attended church weekly, and those who didn't. The Christian guys seemed to feel a much higher degree of responsibility in the area of sex—or at least a greater knowledge of the dynamics and repercussions of sexual involvement. Look at these two comments, from guys in two different church youth groups:

- "For me, even kissing is a huge line I don't want to cross too soon. It's a slippery slope. If I'm kissing, I can go to the next level, and the next. It's like opening up a can of worms. You keep progressing once you open the door."

- "You have to make a line, which is established beforehand. You'll not make a rational decision in the heat of the moment. I tell myself that my hands aren't going to move. I'm not going to think about that. Both of you have to know where the line is, and if a line has been set, you'll have far less of a chance to blow it. You've got to talk beforehand, and if you don't, you almost always lose control. It's easy to lose control."

"If a line has been set, you'll have less of a chance to blow it."

Emotional Fact #2: Having sex doesn't mean he loves you or is committed to you.

You've probably heard this before from your parents or youth group leaders, but now you can hear it from the guys themselves. Those we talked to and surveyed said that for teenage guys, sex usually has little or nothing to do with feeling overwhelming love for their girlfriend, or with wanting any sort of lasting commitment to her.

SURVEY SAYS:

Does moving to a sexually active relationship mean that you want to marry this girl or make a significant life commitment with her?

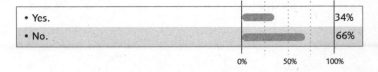

• Yes.	34%
• No.	66%

0%   50%   100%

Two-thirds of the guys confirmed that *sex does not equal significant commitment to that girl.*

This might surprise and alarm some girls, whose major goal is often to secure that loving commitment from a guy. In a girl's mind, the physical element is often an outpouring of love, but guys see things a little differently. Look at these comments from focus groups and the survey:

- "If she says I love you, I'm thinking, 'Really? Can we do it right here and now? Okay!'"

- "Girls use sex to get love, and guys use love to get sex."

- "Just because they say they love you does not mean they do."

One survey-taker gave girls this warning: "Be careful. It's okay to fall in love, but remember that guys usually have other intentions than falling in love. It's very easy to be taken advantage of in today's world. It may not seem like a big deal now to be physical with numerous guys, but you will regret it when you are ready to move on with your life and start a family."

> For teenage guys, sex has little to do with feeling overwhelming love for their girlfriend, or wanting a lasting commitment to her.

Another said: "As a member of the opposite sex I would like to tell girls never to fully trust any guy. As terrible as it sounds, most males in the teenage years don't have much regard for female feelings. There *are* exceptions, so be fair in who you allow into your life—but never assume the one you are with is the exception."

Another guy was blunt: "Guys will say anything to get laid. We'll say, I love you, you're special, whatever it takes. And we might even mean it, but we really mostly mean it for that short time because we're totally focused on what we want."

On the survey, two out of three guys admitted that heavy physical involvement is more about feeling good physically than it is about love.

Whether or not you are currently involved with a girl-friend, if you were to be in a heavy make out situation with a willing partner who was not a long-term girlfriend, what would you primarily be feeling?

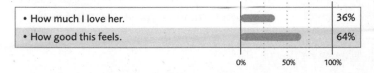

• How much I love her.	36%
• How good this feels.	64%

0%   50%   100%

A guy from a church group told us: "Girls think, 'He's kissing me because he loves me,' whereas in reality, he's usually not."

Almost all the guys we talked to admitted that having sex was not primarily about showing love. And many guys admitted that they could easily make out with a random girl they didn't even know. One guy said, "I'd prefer to make out with someone I cared about, but I'm not opposed to making out with a stranger after a party."

> "Girls think, 'He's kissing me because he loves me,' whereas in reality, he's usually not."

Emotional Fact #3: As soon as you have sex with a guy, he'll likely doubt you.

Okay, here's the result that probably surprises most girls— although not most guys. Although many guys want and will push for some sort of premarital sex, the minute they get it they start to doubt whether the girl can be trusted. And the introduction of that doubt, in turn, undermines the relationship.

SURVEY SAYS:

If you and your partner made the move to a sexual relationship, even if you loved her, would you (or did you) ever find yourself wondering whether you could totally trust her?

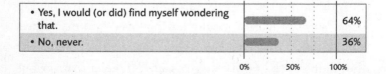

• Yes, I would (or did) find myself wondering that.	64%
• No, never.	36%

0%   50%   100%

Look at these honest comments from the teenage guys we interviewed:

- "If a girl gives in, I don't respect her as much. I find myself wondering about what else she's done in the past."

- "As soon as my girlfriend and I had sex, I knew it was over. I had a feeling it wouldn't work out after that."

- "If she's pushing you into sex, you know you're not the only one."

- "When you're involved physically, the line gets blurred between love and hormones. From then on, you're always wondering which factor is in play. Do I like this girl, or do I just like the physical pleasure? And that confusion totally messes things up."

One guy on the survey gave this insightful warning to teenage girls: "Watch out for guys. Most guys are just out for a quick thrill. Don't give in. See if they are really after you as a person, or just your body. All guys will admit that they don't even *think* about having casual sex with a girl they really like until they are married, because they respect that girl."

To add even more caution, we heard that guilt often

enters the picture after premarital sex and further clouds the couple's future outlook. One young man shared:

> When you have sex with a girl, it can definitely complicate and undermine the relationship. It starts out innocent, and you want it to be innocent, but then you become more sexually active and you realize that things have drifted from the real reason you came together. The sweetness is gone. The sweetness of dating is when the little things can still affect you in a strong way. Like how great it is when she falls asleep on your stomach. It's completely innocent, and that's what it should be about. The more physical stuff can make you feel guilty and undermine the original intent.

Emotional Fact #4:
Guys want to marry a virgin.

Believe it or not, although so many guys want to convince their girlfriends *not* to be a virgin, they want to marry one! This double standard would be amusing if the consequences weren't so serious!

Is the following statement true or false? "I would love to marry a virgin, if possible."

• True.		69%
• False.		31%

As you can see, the overwhelming majority of guys do want to marry a girl who hasn't had a sexual relationship with someone else. Here's what several guys told us:

- "We want a girl without a history because the more guys she's had, the higher the chance that she'll cheat on you."

- "Everyone, if they're honest, wants the virgin."

And yet they see the double standard:

- "Let's be real. How can we say we want the girl to be pure when we're going around [having sex with] every girl and depleting the virgin pool?"

- "We take their virginity and toss them, while still hoping to find a virgin to marry."

- "If you've been an expert at sex, you'll likely convince your virgin girlfriend to go your way. And then where's your virgin?"

> "Everyone,
> if they're honest,
> wants the virgin."

Both religious and non-religious guys want virginity

We found it interesting that both religious guys *and* those who described themselves as non-religious wanted to marry a virgin—although church-goers agreed at much higher rates. Nine out of ten Christian guys—89 percent—wanted to marry a virgin. It was also very important to 59 percent of guys who described themselves as agnostics, atheists, or having no particular religious belief. Here were some of the comments from the guys we interviewed and surveyed—whose religious beliefs were all over the map:

- "Wait until after marriage to have sex. Life is too short to have regrets."

- "I'd love to know that she saved herself for me. That would be so incredible."

- "Breaking chastity after marriage would be a lot more amazing."

And finally, look at this incredible advice one survey-taker offered to teenage girls:

No matter what the guy or your friends tell you, or how cliché this sounds, wait until marriage. Try to think of a more unique gift you can give to your spouse on your honeymoon. Your virginity is the one thing that you can give only once to your spouse. Spend it wisely. And this is coming from a guy, the gender with the reputation for having sex with anything that walks.

The pure in heart

Yet, despite the fact that so many guys wanted a virgin, some qualified their statements in a sweet way:

- "I'd like to marry a virgin, but seeing purity of heart is most important to me. Everyone makes mistakes...I just want to be some girl's hero, even if she's totally blown it. That's how I want to treat my future wife."

- "Purity of heart, or having high moral standards, is a lot stronger of a factor. Especially if they had been really pressured into having sex in a way that was not their fault at all. I definitely value her desire to be pure of heart from this point forward, over a strict definition of virginity."

"Wait until marriage. Your virginity is the one thing that you can give only once to your spouse. Spend it wisely."

WHY IS THIS SUCH AN ISSUE TODAY?

On our survey, half of guys ages fifteen to twenty had already had a sexual relationship—and other surveys have found that the numbers are much higher when guys are specifically asked about oral sex. Many studies show that the trend of unmarried teenage sex is decreasing a bit, which is great. But you will probably agree that half is still too high—especially since that is an average, and the percentage rises significantly among older teens. With both guys and girls *knowing* that there are often negative consequences, why do these high rates exist?

One of the reasons is obvious: Teenagers have strong sex drives and raging hormones. But others aren't quite so obvious. We want to briefly point out some of the less obvious reasons we heard.

Why *he* does it

- **He's constantly being tempted by it.** As you learned in the "visual" chapter, the sight of exciting visual images sexually stimulates a guy. Well, think about it. In this culture, that basically means his sex drive is being kicked into overdrive all the time, every time he watches television and every time he walks through the mall—or the school. If he is constantly being tempted by sex, it's not surprising that that temptation would seem increasingly difficult to resist.

- **Peer pressure creates internal pressure.** We all know there's a lot of locker-room bragging among guys about their "conquests"—even if it's totally untrue. This peer pressure actually creates an internal pressure for a guy. As one said, "Guys can be merciless toward each other. They'll say, 'What? You haven't scored with her yet? What's wrong with you, man?' And then, despite yourself, you might start thinking something is wrong with you." (As a matter of fact, while we were finishing up this book, a guy who knows sixteen-year-old Sarah informed her that he couldn't believe he was seventeen and hadn't gotten laid yet, and *she* was the lucky girl he had picked to relieve him of his virginity. No pretense of love…just to relieve the peer pressure. She, we are glad to report, told him to get lost!)

- **Once it's on his mind (which is a lot of the time), hormones can override his brain.** The guys told us that in the heat of the moment, they just plain *want* to give in—even if they know they shouldn't. So unless girls can help them stop, they will want to keep going.

Why *she* does it

Girls also have sex drives and hormones, even if they aren't always as assertive as a guy's during the teen years. In addition to the physical pleasure part of it, girls often engage in sex to feel close to a guy, to fill an emotional need, rather than just a physical one. In *Sisterhood of the Traveling Pants*, Bridget pursues a sexual relationship with the coach because she needs to feel loved and accepted, whereas the coach gives in because a hot girl is after him and it feels good to finally give in.

> Girls often engage in sex to feel close to a guy, to fill an emotional need, rather than just a physical one.

There are other issues that girls, especially, need to watch out for. Dr. Julie Carberry, an Atlanta-based psychologist specializing in counseling teens, gave us this additional insight:

I've seen that many girls feel it's their God-given role to rescue guys. For example, a good Christian girl might feel compelled to always be that listening ear, that need-meeter. Especially with a guy, a girl might feel that she "should" also meet his "sexual needs." When a girl loses her emotional boundaries, she often loses her sexual boundaries as well.

The problem, of course, is that losing those boundaries and giving in often sets in motion the negative emotional consequences—such as the guy no longer trusting the girl—that undermine the terrific relationship that both parties probably would have preferred.

GUYS WANT YOUR HELP TO AVOID NEGATIVE CONSEQUENCES!

So many guys we talked to were clearly good guys who didn't want to ruin their relationships. They didn't want the negative consequences of having a sexual relationship before marriage. But because they also had such powerful physical urges, they said they needed their girlfriend's help in keeping the relationship safely on the "innocent" side of the line.

Look at these comments about how guys *know* there are emotional consequences:

- "I know that sex is playing with a girl's emotions... and it's selfish. It will always result in something bad."

- "Guys know that we can forever damage a girl."

And this advice from a survey-taker:

- "Don't have sex! Stop and imagine the consequences. I can tell you, it brings problems!"

At the same time, we heard many guys express their beliefs—or fears—that limiting the physical, sexual progression was all up to them. They wanted the girl to help, wanted her to help set the standards for how far things would go, as a protection against those times when both were feeling weak.

So, since they want your help, what would that look like? What we heard fell into several categories.

Set boundaries!

Almost every guy who felt some responsibility to not go "too far" believed it was critical to set boundaries. (Not to mention the even *greater* need for boundaries with guys who say that how far they go is entirely up to the girl!) Among the more responsible guys, if they didn't know where their girls stood, it weakened their resolve to not go too far.

As one guy said, "I'm never quite sure how far to take things with a girl if we haven't discussed our limits beforehand. It's kind of awkward to actually talk about limits when you're in a new relationship. But you've got to."

On the survey, one guy's advice to teen girls was clear: "Make sure that you set boundaries and stick to them. Don't let a guy go farther or faster than what you are comfortable with. Don't assume that having fun making out means that the feeling is love. The word *love* is used too much nowadays. Don't bounce from one relationship to another. Sometimes, being single is all right."

Don't assume Christian guys are immune.

Despite the fact that Christian guys had tighter standards, several expressed the pressure they felt to be totally different than the guys in the world. They want girls to know that guys are all wired *the same way*. Just because they have a strong commitment to their faith doesn't mean they're not bombarded with the same temptations as every other guy. They worry that many Christian girls have the wrong perception that godliness means there are no impure thoughts or sexual desires.

> Guys worry that girls have the wrong perception that godliness means there are no impure thoughts or sexual desires.

This fact was illustrated recently with a friend of mine. Her daughter was wearing shorts and doing some stretches in the gym one day, when her mother saw her and pulled her aside. She told her daughter, "Be careful about your stretches because people can see your underwear. There's a whole team of basketball players over there, watching you." Her daughter said, "Mom, you don't have to worry. This is a Christian school, and those are Christian guys. They wouldn't think that way."

As the Christian guys themselves told us, "Oh, yes they would!"

Do a Joseph!

On many subjects, the Bible says to "stand strong," to hold firmly to your beliefs, to be steadfast. But in the area of sexual temptation, the Bible instead says, *"Run!"* God knows that once we are in a difficult situation, it is that much more difficult to get out. So He tells us to avoid sexual temptation at all costs, and where it has snuck up on us, to run as far and fast as we can. The Bible actually says, *"Flee* from sexual immorality."

One youth pastor we know talks about fleeing temptation with the saying, "Do a Joseph!" In the Old Testament there is a great story about a handsome young man named Joseph, who was being pursued by his boss's wife. She would constantly ask him to sleep with her, and you can imagine the temptation this must have been! One day she even physically grabbed him, and he broke free and ran away in such a hurry he left his shirt behind. Why did he run? It's not like she could *make* him have sex with her, right? No... he ran because he knew he had to get out of that incredibly tempting situation *now!*

So many of the guys we talked to said that is exactly the case for them. The further they go sexually, the more difficult it is to run. So if you find yourself in a place of strong temptation, we urge you to "do a Joseph," and run! Help your guy protect both of you from hurting each other, your relationship, your future, and your relationship with God.

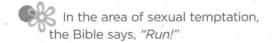 In the area of sexual temptation, the Bible says, *"Run!"*

Please don't rely on the guy you are with, no matter how honorable he is. Remember, he's being tempted, too. Instead, cry out to God for the way of escape that He promises is there. First Corinthians 10:13 says, "With the temptation [He] will provide the way of escape" (NASB).

We have found that this prayer works in *any* temptation: "Lord God, I'm being tempted by _____, and I'm asking for your promised way of escape. You've promised to provide it; now show it to me! I don't want to fall!" This type of prayer puts the burden on God, but guess what? He can handle it.

THE GUY WANTS TO BE YOUR HERO...NOT YOUR HINDRANCE

Almost all the guys we talked to said that when they weren't in the heat of the moment, they really did want to be a girl's hero, and not create a hindrance that would cause regret later. They spoke about their desire to be romantic, to have honor and true friendship in their dating relationships. So many guys want to find the right girl in the right time, and to have the relationship God intended. And they know that until then, each relationship brings them one step closer to that day—and they want to handle it well.

Look at these great quotes from the guys:

- "I just want to be some girl's hero."

- "The goal of dating is, eventually, marriage. And even when a guy gets married, there are always going to be temptations. I want to keep myself from 'looking' right now because down the road that habit could really hurt. I'm practicing commitment right now, while I'm young."

- "I love it best when she just puts her head on my shoulder. Feeling her hair on the back of my neck is so great; it's all I need right now. I want to maintain the innocence of this level."

- "I like the sweet gestures, well under the line of being sexually active."

One of the survey-takers had this advice for all you girls:

I would tell them that not all guys are out for just sex.
That is a major stereotype. There are a lot of guys
that are there for the relationship and they like to
build that relationship. So don't go around selling
yourself just because that is what you think you
should be doing. The right guy will come eventually.

Another said: "Think about what you are doing now...it
will be with you forever."

It should truly bring hope to know that so many of the
guys we interviewed were romantic, idealistic, and cared
about the girls in their life. Wait for one like that—one who
will honor you enough to want to wait until you are married.

If you've blown it, ask for a "Do-Over"

If you have blown it in this area, remember that God gives
us "Do-Overs." Trust Him with your past, and ask Him for a
clean slate for the future.

One guy we spoke to had a message for those of you in
this situation: "For those who have already given away their

virginity: You can still wait with the next guy. You can start over, and the two of you can wait together. It'll be worth it."

In closing...

Realize that God has a solution for the sexual pressures everyone feels. The same God who created sex also devised a plan to enjoy this gift in the right way and in the right place—in the context of marriage, where the stirring of all those desires creates not distrust and guilt and shame, but delight. Remember, God always has the perfect time, place, and way to fulfill every desire within your heart.

If your parents have been after you to reserve sex for marriage, some of you might be tempted to think, *They just don't know what pressure we face today.* Well, as parents ourselves, we can tell you—without getting into detail we wouldn't want our daughters to read!—that you're wrong. We do know exactly the pressure you face, because we faced the exact same thing.

More important, though, is that *God* does indeed realize what century you live in. That fact has not somehow escaped Him! And He says He provides a way of escape for *every temptation.*

You can count on that, no matter what. The desires you have are God-given, and the desires God gives you are the desires He will find a way to fulfill for you.

Chapter 8

WORDS FOR YOUR HEART

What Guys *Really* Want To Tell You

We've come almost to the end of our journey together. But before we get to the final, most important revelation about how guys think, we want to share something from our hearts as we walk this path with you.

Some of you may be challenged by what you've learned in these pages. These realities may not fit what you have always thought. But just as we have discussed the difficult choices we expect our guys to make, we have to make our own. We can remain behind our idealistic wishes about how guys "should be," or we can step out and face the truth—and all that it means for us.

We hope and pray you'll accept this call to maturity and

receive this invitation for your generation to become the strong, gentle, godly young women that you are intended to be—not just with the guys you know today, but on into your future as well. If you are willing to be molded by His hands, the Lord will shower you and your relationships with abundance. That is the way He works, because you are precious to Him.

> We can remain behind our idealistic wishes about how guys "should be," or we can step out and face the truth—and all that it means for us.

And that brings us to the conclusion of our journey—the single most important thing you need to know about the inner lives of young men…the survey response that most surprised and delighted us.

THE NUMBER ONE SURVEY RESPONSE

As you now know, at the end of the survey we gave the guys a blank space and asked one open-ended question that they could answer however they wanted:

Imagine that there is an auditorium full of teenage girls, including your little sister, and you have been asked to give these girls your advice about moving forward in a world of guys. You are behind a curtain, so you're totally anonymous. What's your best heart-to-heart advice for them?

Hundreds of responses rolled in, and by far the top thing the guys wanted to tell girls was this:

Be yourself, because you are more valuable than you think.

We were stunned. Because the survey polled every conceivable type of teenage guy around the country, in all honesty we were expecting a high number of flippant or even raunchy comments—and yes, we did get some of those, too! But by far the largest number of responses were from teen guys speaking directly to each teen girl and telling her that she has worth, that she is valuable—and encouraging her to break free from the pressure to be someone she is not or to do something she doesn't want to do. Over and over, the guys summed it up by saying, "Just be yourself."

We could fill up five pages with the wonderful responses we got, but since our space is limited, here is just a taste of what these guys wanted to share with you. (Many of the other comments are available at our website, www.foryoungwomenonly.com).

- "Be who you are and do what you think is right, not what others want you to do."

- "Be yourself."

- "Be yourself and don't feel like you have to act like everyone else."

- "Be yourself! Don't act different to get us to like you."

- "Be yourself. Don't try to mold yourself into the image society creates. That way, when you find that perfect guy you'll know he likes you for who you really are."

- "Don't be afraid to be yourself. If they don't like you for you, then they aren't worth your time. Have fun together but don't forget about your friends, because the guys will come and go but your friends will always be there in the end."

> Over and over, the guys summed it up by saying, "Just be yourself."

- "Give guys a chance. We are just as inexperienced as you. And don't act like someone you're not to impress us. If you don't feel comfortable with having a sexual relationship, then tell us. Most of us would be okay with that—and if we aren't then you don't need to be involved with us anyway."

- "Have respect for yourself."

- "If you respect yourself, for the most part guys should respect you."

- "Just be confident and be yourself, and guys will like you."

- "Just be yourself."

- "Just be yourself and things will work out ok."

- "Just be yourself! You don't have to change yourself to get guys. The guys are the ones that should change for a girl...we should be glad you girls exist.

- "Never compromise your principles."

- "Never give up, and don't let people say you can't do something just because you're a girl and that's supposedly a man's job."

- "Never lose sight of who you truly are and what your own hopes and dreams are."

- "No matter what, just be yourself."

In keeping with those "be yourself" comments, there were other, equally encouraging themes that emerged from the guys we surveyed and interviewed on that question.

Understand your identity.

In our focus groups of Christian guys, many of the guys challenged and encouraged girls to not only be themselves, but to accept who they are as children of God. If this is a new concept for you, we would encourage you to ask a Christian friend or pastor what it means to be a child of God, and to draw your identity solely from Him as your heavenly Father. As one guy put it:

> Understand your true identity. Before you can understand who you are, you must know who Christ is. Good grades, college, and relationships will all fall short if you're not in God's purposes. They'll never be fully realized.

Another one put it this way: "You're more valuable than you think. You don't have to dress a certain way or perform a certain way to have value. You were lovingly created by a God who adores you."

Be confident in who you are.

The guys also spoke a lot about the importance of girls developing *confidence* in their identity, and realizing they are special just as they are. As one survey-taker said:

> Honestly, I would teach girls to be confident. Girls are still brought up seeing tall lanky supermodels being called beautiful, and they believe that if they don't look the same way they're ugly. Women need to be more confident, whether that is confidence in their appearance or even in their ability to talk to a guy. A girl who knows what she wants and isn't afraid to show it is the most appealing girl of all.

"You're more valuable than you think. You were lovingly created by a God who adores you."

Think about the big picture.

That said, many teenage guys acknowledged how hard it is to *keep* a godly identity these days. They said that they know just how much pressure girls face—including pressure from *them!* But as we said in the last chapter, one of the strongest themes that emerged on the survey and in our interviews was guys wanting to tell girls not to give in to that pressure.

When the guys were anonymously sharing advice as they would with a good female friend, the vast majority of them were protective, wanting to make sure you would have no regrets. One teenager asked the girls reading this book to think about the big picture:

> I often think about what my pastor, Andy Stanley, has advised about handling the pressure to give in to all the temptations we face. In those heat-of-the-moment decisions, think about how everything will end up as a story, years down the road. Think about how you want to tell the story...and how you want to be personified in it. Do you want to be the hero...or embarrassed?

Others said similar things:

- "I dare you to live. Don't look back and look on all the opportunities where you didn't step out. Live from your heart. You know what you want to do.... Do it."

- "Don't hold back your potential for another person. You have to be effective by yourself first."

- "It's not about the here and now. You're in school to learn and prepare for the future. A lot of girls base their biggest decisions on today's circumstances...on the best friend they're never gonna see after high school. They kiss a guy they shouldn't have just because he thought it was cool. Get out of the now thinking and into the future."

- "Friends and boyfriends are for a season. Don't sacrifice the most important things of all for the friends you think are so important now."

THE FUTURE IS NOT FAR OFF

We hope that what you have learned about guys has challenged you to think about what it means for *you*. As we said at the very beginning, the point of all this is not just for you to learn fun, fascinating facts, but to grow and mature in any areas you think you need to work on. And what you learn about how to relate well to guys now will carry through into all your future relationships—including with your future husband.

Recognizing this reality, one guy on the survey shared this advice straight from the heart:

Be honest with guys and tell them how you feel. Be loyal to them and don't take advantage of them. Treat them kindly and don't put yourself in a situation to make their trust in you falter.

> What you learn about guys now will carry through into all your future relationships

In conclusion, one guy we talked to provided great encouragement to every girl who's been disillusioned by the apparent immaturity and shortsightedness of the males in her life. We interviewed him because at twenty-two, he was just out of college, and a newlywed. He shared this thought with all the girls out there who want to be strong, godly young women but also want to find someone to love:

When we are in school, most of us—guys or girls—have no idea what love really is. Love really and truly is waking up with your wife in the middle of the night when she's sick. Holding the bucket because she's throwing up. In school, it's all about emotion and status. It's all about how this beautiful girl or guy likes me. We just don't comprehend what it means when we're young...that it's a sacrifice. True love forces you to see your own selfishness—and get past it. That's where the happiness lies. And oh, man, it's worth waiting for.

Realize that even as you read these chapters and work on yourself, that God is working, too. He is working not just to help you, but also to mold the guys you know into selfless, sacrificial, Christ-like young men who will one day make amazing husbands.

We hope that you can catch the vision of what that looks like—and that it truly is worth waiting for.

A Note to the Reader

If what you have read has been helpful, we hope you are eager to learn more. You can find other resources—including the entire survey, online forums, and other fun resources—at our website for this book, www.foryoungwomenonly.com.

WHERE ALL THIS RESEARCH CAME FROM

After more than a year of formulating surveys, conducting focus groups, interviewing "guys on the street" and putting our findings to pen and paper (well, okay, computer), we're amazed as we look back and consider all the thousands of people and resources who made this book possible. It would be impossible to thank them all, but we need to highlight a few—and we beg forgiveness in advance from anyone that our sleep-deprived brains have left out!

Citations

We use illustrations from several movies and TV shows including (in alphabetical order):

- *Agent Cody Banks*, directed by Harald Zwart (MGM, 2003). Cast: Frankie Muniz, Hilary Duff, Angie Harmon, and Keith David.

- *The Incredibles*, directed by Brad Bird (Pixar, 2004).

- *Mean Girls*, directed by Mark Waters (Paramount, 2004). Cast: Lindsay Lohan, Rachel McAdams, Tina Fey, and Tim Meadows.

- *Seinfeld* TV series (Castle Rock Entertainment/NBC, 1990–1998). Cast: Jerry Seinfeld, Julia Louis-Dreyfus, Michael Richards, and Jason Alexander.

- *Shallow Hal*, directed by Bobby Farrelly and Peter Farrelly (20th Century Fox, 2001). Cast: Gwyneth Paltrow, Jack Black, Jason Alexander, and Joe Viterelli.

- *The Sisterhood of the Traveling Pants*, directed by Ken Kwapis (Warner Bros., 2005). Cast: Amber Tamblyn, Alexis Bledel, America Ferrera, Blake Lively, and Jenna Boyd.

- *Spider-Man 2*, directed by Sam Raimi (Columbia Pictures, 2004). Cast: Tobey Maguire and Kirsten Dunst.

- *Star Trek: The Next Generation* TV series, created by Gene Roddenberry (Paramount, 1987–1994), episode #260, "Attached."

- A *Walk to Remember*, directed by Adam Shankman (Warner Bros, 2002) Cast: Shane West and Mandy Moore.

Several experts were invaluable in actively providing insight and help as we investigated these topics, for our "Ask the Expert" sections, and elsewhere:

- Chapter 2: Dr. Emerson Eggerichs, founder of Love and Respect Ministries and author of *Love and Respect* (Integrity, 2004).

- Chapter 4: Clayton S. Kull, L.C.S.W., and Cheryl Kull, both parents, counselors, and ordained ministers, Atlanta, Georgia.

- Chapter 5: Vicki Courtney, founder of VirtuousReality.com, national speaker, and bestselling author of *TeenVirtue: Real Issues, Real Life…A Teen Girl's Survival Guide*.

- Chapter 5: Daniel Weiss, senior analyst for media and sexuality, Focus on the Family.

- Chapter 6: Dr. Linda Mintle, body image psychologist and author of *Overweight Kids* (Integrity, 2005), www.drlinda-helps.com.

- Chapter 7: Julie Carbery, Ph.D., developmental child and family counselor, and college adjunct faculty.

Acknowledgments

During this long process, several teams of people covered the whole process in prayer. We are so incredibly grateful these dear people, including:

Martha and Barry Abrams, Kurt Alme, Diana Baker, Elizabeth Beinhocker, Julie Blount, David and Linda Boris, Michael and Deon Brown, Anne Browne, Kathy Carnahan, Mark and Christa Crawford, Gerry and Kasey Crete, Linda Crews, Alison Darrell, Mike Degle, Zanese Duncan, Betty Dunkum, Calvin Edwards, Craig and Lynn Elam, Mollianne Elliott, Julie Fidler, Darby Ferguson, Susan Fleck, Larissa Fontenot, Nancy French, Lisa and Ron Fry, Natt and Meredith Gantt, Kate Gates, Dan Glaze, Michael and Debra Goldstone, Jennifer Graves, Laura Grindley, Dean and Jan Harbry, Judy Hitson, John and Monica Holcomb, Lin Hopkins, Anne Hotchkiss, Victor Jih, Jane Joiner, Audrey Lambert, Kristen Lambert, Mary Laudermil, Charl and Elsa Liebenberg, Jan and John MacLaury, Karen McAdams, Jurt Montavon, Lisa and John Nagle, Bruce and Sue Osterink, Darlene Penner, Elizabeth Noller, Linda and Jack Preston, Dick and Judy Reidinger, Melba Rice, Annabelle Robertson, Phil and Susan Rodenberg, Andy and Jeanne Sandecki, Roger Scarlett, Albert and Wendy Shashoua, Jim and Chris Sharp, Jenny Shea, Barry and Janet Smith, D.J. Snell, JoAnn Turbie, Lon and Katherine Waitman, and Ed and Jewels Warren. Thanks also to the many, many faithful members of the prayer team of interested readers, who have been led to come alongside in prayer as well.

For the third time, our deep thanks to Chuck Cowan of Analytic Focus (www.analyticfocus.com), who helped us design a stellar national survey, which was then conducted by the skillful team of Jim Nelems at the Marketing Workshop in Atlanta, Georgia (www.mwshop.com). The world needs more people who dot every "i" and cross every "t" to make things right.

We promised to keep the full names of the interviewees and focus group participants confidential, but we would like to thank, by first name only, several of the Atlanta-based focus group guys, who not only provided great initial insights, but who allowed us to go back to them with questions, questions, and more questions: Adam, Andrew, Bryan, Charlie Chip, Chris, Dan, David, Devin, Eric, Frank, Greg, James, Jered, John, Jonathan, the other Jonathan, Joseph, Kent, Kristopher, Larry, Matt, Nate, Nathan, Robbie, Ross, Stephen, Yotam, and Zachary. Special thanks to Marsha Anderson-Bomar, who graciously allowed us the use of her offices at Street Smarts to host several focus groups.

We could not have written this book without the personal and professional assistance of Shaunti's hardworking staff team, including Vance Hanifen, Jeanne Sandecki, Maylynn Wilson, and most especially her "right-hand man," Linda Crews. Thanks also to Zanese Duncan for her dedicated help in approaching potential endorsers. And, as always, we deeply appreciate the incredible insight and encouragement of our agent, Calvin Edwards.

We owe extreme gratitude to the tireless and talented efforts of our editors, Lisa Bowden and David Kopp, who applied their magic touches to our findings—even past the eleventh hour—on weekends and through sickness! We also appreciate Danae Yankoski's wonderful editorial insight. And our deepest thanks to Don Jacobson and the whole Multnomah family for their spirit of excellence and grace—especially with high-maintenance authors like us!

Our undying gratitude also goes out to our parents, Richard and Judy Reidinger and Glen and Lee Hultquist, who beautifully modeled so many of the positive principles we're highlighting in this book. We're so grateful for your influence and continued encouragement. Also, special thanks to Sarah and Hannah Rice, whose input was invaluable…especially your efforts to help us come across as more cool than we actually are. We'd also like to thank Brandon Rice and the Feldhahn kids, all of whom had to put their wishes and schedules on hold several times to accommodate this work.

There's no way we can adequately express our thanks to our husbands, Jeff Feldhahn and Eric Rice, two amazing, godly guys who saw past our weaknesses and sought out "diamonds in the rough" when they found us in school. We can't imagine undertaking this without your incredible support, constant encouragement, and timely wisdom.

Finally, the highest glory and praise goes to God, who gave us the idea for the book, and whose Spirit blew past the furniture of our history and abilities to create what He needed in this book for the teens He so loves.

Blessings to you all!

—Shaunti & Lisa

If you want even more information about how guys think, be sure to visit our website!

ForYoungWomenOnly.com contains exclusive content not found anywhere else, including:

* The entire survey, including questions not discussed in the book

* The word-for-word comments of hundreds of guys who were asked, "What is the one thing you would advise girls about going forward in a world of guys?"

* Recommended resources

You can find new stuff all the time, including:

* Exclusive articles by several key experts

* Online forums for additional discussion, including online chat sessions with Shaunti and the guys she interviewed

* "Ask Matt"—a chance for girls to ask questions and get answers from a normal Christian guy who is willing to share from his heart

Join us today as we continue to find out what makes guys tick!

foryoungwomenonly.com

Also from **Shaunti Feldhahn**

From the author who started it all, Shaunti Feldhahn brings women life-changing resources to take the guesswork out of relating to your man. Surprising, eye-popping truths on every page!

For Women Only

What's going on in a man's mind? Take a look into the inner lives of men, and find guidance in providing the loving support that they want and need!

For Women Only 1-59052-317-2
Discussion Guide 1-59052-768-2
Audio CD 1-59052-574-4

www.forwomenonlybook.com

For Parents Only
Coming May 2007!

For every bewildered parent, there is a teenager or younger child just longing to be understood. What does a son need from his mom? How should a dad relate to his daughter? **Bestselling author Shaunti Feldhahn again joins Lisa Rice in helping moms and dads understand things they just don't 'get' about the inner workings of sons and daughters.** This book is every parent's simple, straightforward guide to understanding how their kids are wired, and loving them in the way they need. 1-59052-932-4

Want to be reminded when this book comes out?
Log on to www.mpbooks.com/FPO
and enter an e-mail address where we can reach you.

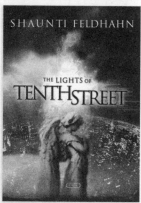